Improve your Communication Skills

D0839300

Improve your Communication Skills

Alan Barker | Revised Second Edition

KoganPage

LONDON PHILADELPHIA NEW DELHI

Publisher's note
Every possible effort has been made to ensure that the information contained in this book is accurate at the time of going to press, and the publishers and author cannot accept responsibility for any errors or omissions, however caused. No responsibility for loss or damage occasioned to any person acting, or refraining from action, as a result of the material in this publication can be accepted by the editor, the publisher or the author.

First published 2000
Second edition 2006
Reprinted 2007 (twice)
Revised second edition 2010

120 Pentonville Road	525 South 4th Street, #241	4737/23 Ansari Road
London N1 9JN	Philadelphia PA 19147	Daryaganj
United Kingdom	USA	New Delhi 110002
www.koganpage.com		India

© Alan Barker 2000, 2006, 2010

The right of Alan Barker to be identified as the author of this work has been asserted by him in accordance with the Copyright, Designs and Patents Act 1988.

ISBN   978 0 7494 6036 5
E-ISBN   978 0 7494 5911 6

British Library Cataloguing-in-Publication Data

A CIP record for this book is available from the British Library.

Library of Congress Cataloging-in-Publication Data

Barker, Alan, 1956–
    Improve your communication skills / Alan Barker. -- Rev. 2nd ed.
        p. cm.
    ISBN 978-0-7494-5627-6 -- ISBN 978-0-7494-5911-6 (e-bk) 1. Business communication. I. Title.
    HF5718.B365 2010
    651.7--dc22
                                                        2009043350

Typeset by Jean Cussons Typesetting, Diss, Norfolk
Printed and bound in India by Replika Press Pvt Ltd

Contents

About this book

If you're not communicating, you're not managing. In 2003, the American Management Association asked its members what skills go to make an effective leader. Number one skill – way ahead of the others – was communication (84 per cent). Interestingly, numbers two and three – motivating others (56 per cent) and team-building (46 per cent) – also rely on effective communication. What's more, 60 per cent of executives who responded listed lack of collaboration as their top leadership challenge.

Management is no longer a matter of command and control. Managers must now work with matrix management and networking, with outsourcing and partnerships. We must influence people to act, often without being able to wield power over them. Our success depends, more than ever before, on other people.

The new technologies have been a mixed blessing. IT helps us keep in touch but can reduce our opportunities to talk to each other. Many of us have become 'cubicle workers', spending most of our day interfacing with a computer screen.

Corporate communication can, of course, still be remarkably

effective. The MD's efforts to communicate his latest corporate change programme may fall at the first hurdle; but rumours of imminent job losses can spread like wildfire. If only formal communication could achieve half the success of gossip!

Our organisations are networks of conversations. The unit of management work is the conversation; and the quality of our work depends directly on the quality of our conversations. How can we communicate more effectively? How can we begin to improve the quality of our conversations at work? This book seeks to answer those questions.

1

What is communication?

It's a question I often ask at the start of training courses. How would you define the word 'communication'?

After a little thought, most people come up with a sentence like this.

> **Communication is the act of transmitting and receiving information.**

This definition appears very frequently. We seem to take it for granted. Where does it come from? And does it actually explain how we communicate at work?

The transmission model

That word 'transmitting' suggests that we tend to think of communication as a technical process. And the history of the word 'communication' supports that idea.

In the 19th century, the word 'communication' came to refer to the movement of goods and people, as well as of information. We still use the word in these ways, of course: roads and railways are forms of communication, just as much as speaking or writing. And we still use the images of the industrial revolution – the canal, the railway and the postal service – to describe human communication. Information, like freight, comes in 'bits'; it needs to be stored, transferred and retrieved. And we describe the movement of information in terms of a 'channel', along which information 'flows'.

This transport metaphor was readily adapted to the new, electronic technologies of the 20th century. We talk about 'telephone lines' and 'television channels'. Electronic information comes in 'bits', stored in 'files' or 'vaults'. The words 'download' and 'upload' use the freight metaphor; e-mail uses postal imagery.

In 1949, Claude Shannon and Warren Weaver published a formal version of the transmission model (Shannon, Claude E and Weaver, Warren, *A Mathematical Model of Communication*, University of Illinois Press, Urbana, IL, 1949). Shannon and Weaver were engineers working for Bell Telephone Labs in the United States. Their goal was to make telephone cables as efficient as possible.

Their model had five elements:

- an *information source*, which produces a message;
- a *transmitter*, which encodes the message into signals;
- a *channel*, to which signals are adapted for transmission;
- a *receiver*, which decodes the message from the signal; and
- a *destination*, where the message arrives.

They introduced a sixth element, *noise:* any interference with the message travelling along the channel (such as 'static' on the telephone or radio) that might alter the message being sent. A final element, feedback, was introduced in the 1950s.

Figure 1.1   The Shannon–Weaver transmission model of communication

For the telephone, the channel is a wire, the signal is an electrical current, and the transmitter and receiver are the handsets. Noise would include crackling from the wire. Feedback would include the dialling tone, which tells you that the line is 'live'.

In a conversation, my brain is the source and your brain is the receiver. The encoder might be the language I use to speak with you; the decoder is the language you use to understand me. Noise would include any distraction you might experience as I speak. Feedback would include your responses to what I am saying: gestures, facial expressions and any other signals I pick up that give me some sense of how you are receiving my message.

We also apply the transmission metaphor to human communication. We 'have' an idea (as if it were an object). We 'put the idea into words' (like putting it into a box); we try to 'put our idea across' (by pushing it or 'conveying' it); and the 'receiver' – hopefully – 'gets' the idea. We may need to 'unpack' the idea before the receiver can 'grasp' it. Of course, we need to be careful to avoid 'information overload'.

The transmission model is attractive. It suggests that

information is objective and quantifiable: something that you and I will always understand in exactly the same way. It makes communication seem measurable, predictable and consistent: sending an e-mail seems to be evidence that I have communicated to you. Above all, the model is simple: we can draw a diagram to illustrate it.

But is the transmission model accurate? Does it reflect what actually happens when people communicate with each other? And, if it's so easy to understand, why does communication – especially in organisations – so often go wrong?

Wiio's Laws

We all know that communication in organisations is notoriously unreliable. Otto Wiio (born 1928) is a Finnish Professor of Human Communication. He is best known for a set of humorous maxims about how communication in organisations goes wrong. They illustrate some of the problems of using the transmission model.

Communication usually fails, except by accident.

If communication can fail, it will fail.

If communication cannot fail, it still usually fails.

If communication seems to succeed in the way you intend – someone's misunderstood.

If you are content with your message, communication is certainly failing.

If a message can be interpreted in several ways, it will be interpreted in a manner that maximises the damage.

There is always someone who knows better than you what your message means.

The more we communicate, the more communication fails.

Problems with the transmission model

What's wrong with the transmission model? Well, to begin with, a message differs from a parcel in a very obvious way. When I send the parcel, I no longer have it; when I send a message, I still have it. But the metaphor throws up some other interesting, rather more subtle problems.

Do we communicate what we intend?

The transmission model assumes that communication is always intentional: that the sender always communicates for a purpose, and always knows what that purpose is. In fact, most human communication mixes the intentional and the unintentional. We all know that we communicate a great deal without meaning to, through body language, eye movement and tone of voice.

The transmission model also assumes that the intention and the communication are separate. First we have a thought; then we decide how to encode it. In reality, we may not know what we are thinking until we have said it; the act of encoding is the process of thinking. Many writers, for example, say that they write *in order to* work out what their ideas are.

What's the context?

A message delivered by post will have a very different effect to a message delivered vocally, face-to-face. Our response to the message will differ if it's delivered by a senior manager or by a colleague. Our state of mind when we hear or read the message will affect how we understand it. And so on.

A one-way street

The transmission model is a linear. The source actively sends a message; the destination passively receives it. The model ignores the active participation of the 'receiver' in generating the meaning of the communication.

What does it all mean?

The transmission model ignores the way humans understand. Human beings don't process information; they process meanings.

For example, the words 'I'm fine' could mean:

- **'I am feeling well';**
- **'I am happy';**
- **'I was feeling unwell but am now feeling better';**
- **'I was feeling unhappy but now feel less unhappy';**
- **'I am not injured; there's no need to help me';**
- **'Actually, I feel lousy but I don't want you to know it';**
- **'Help!'**

– or any one of a dozen other ideas. The receiver has to understand the meaning of the words if they are to respond appropriately; but the words may not contain the speaker's whole meaning.

> **There is a paradox in communicating. I cannot expect that you will understand _everything_ I tell you; and I cannot expect that you will understand _only_ what I tell you.**
> (with thanks to Patrick Bouvard)

If we want to develop our communication skills, we need to move beyond the transmission model. We need to think about communication in a new way. And that means thinking about how we understand.

Understanding how we understand

Understanding is essentially a pattern-matching process. We create meaning by matching external stimuli from our environment to mental patterns inside our brains. The human brain is the most complex system we know of. It contains 100 billion neurons (think of a neuron as a kind of switch). The power of the brain lies in its networking capacity. The brain groups neurons into networks that 'switch on' during certain mental activities. These networks are infinitely flexible: we can alter existing networks, and grow new ones. The number of possible neural networks in one brain easily exceeds the number of particles in the known universe.

The brain is a mighty networker; but it is also an amazing processor. My computer is a serial processor: it can only do one thing at a time. We can describe the brain as a parallel processor. It can work on many things at once. If one neural circuit finishes before another, it sends the information to other networks so that they can start to use it.

Parallel processing allows the brain to develop a very dynamic relationship with reality. Think of it as 'bottom-up' processing and 'top-down' processing.

- *Bottom-up processing*: **The brain doesn't recognise objects directly. It looks for features, such as shape and colour. The networks that look for features operate independently of each other, and in parallel. 'Bottom-up' processing occurs, appropriately, in the lower – and more primitive – parts of the brain, including the brain stem and the cerebellum. The neural networks in these regions send information upwards, into the higher regions of the brain: the neo-cortex.**
- *Top-down processing*: **Meanwhile, the higher-level centres of the brain – in the neo-cortex, sitting above and around the lower parts of the brain – are doing 'top-down' processing: providing the mental networks**

that organise information into patterns and give it meaning. As you read, for example, bottom-up processing recognises the shapes of letters; top-down processing provides the networks to combine the shapes into the patterns of recognisable words.

When the elements processed bottom-up have been matched against the patterns supplied by top-down processing, the brain has understood what's out there.

Top-down and bottom-up processing engage in continuous, mutual feedback. It's a kind of internal conversation within the brain. Bottom-up processing constantly sends new information upwards so that the higher regions can update and adjust their neural networks. Meanwhile, top-down processing constantly organises incoming information into new or existing patterns.

The brain often has to make a calculated guess about what it has perceived. Incoming information is often garbled, ambiguous or incomplete. How can my brain distinguish your voice from all the other noise in a crowded room? Or a flower from a picture of a flower? How does it recognise a tune from just a few notes?

Top-down processing often completes incoming information by using pre-existing patterns. The brain creates a *mental model*: a representation of reality, created by matching incomplete information to learned patterns in the brain.

Visual illusions demonstrate how the brain makes these calculated guesses. In the image in Figure 1.2, for example, we appear to see a white triangle, even though the image contains no triangle. The brain's top-down processing completes the incoming information by imposing a 'triangle' pattern – its best guess of what is there. (The triangle is named after Gaetano Kanizsa, an Italian psychologist and artist, founder of the Institute of Psychology of Trieste.)

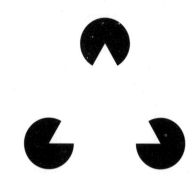

Figure 1.2 A Kanizsa triangle

We can call this process 'perceptual completion', and it's not limited to visual information. Perceptual completion shows that all understanding is a 'best guess'.

A new model of communication

What does all this mean for communication?

To begin with, the most important question we can ask when we are communicating is:

'What effect am I having?'

How does the information we are giving relate to the other person's mental models? What meaning do they attach to our behaviour, our words, gestures and voice?

But we can go further. The pattern-matching model of communication suggests three important principles.

First, communication is continuous. If we are always updating our understanding, then communication needs to be continuous to be effective: not a one-off event, like a radio transmission, but a process.

Second, communication is complicated. Whatever we understand, has been communicated. That means everything we observe: not just the words someone speaks, but the music of their voice and the dance of their body. Some of the signals we send out are intentional; very many are not. We communicate *if we are being observed.*

> **We cannot *not* communicate.**
> (Paul Watzlawick, Mental Research Institute, Palo Alto, California)

Third, communication is contextual. It never happens in isolation. The meaning of the communication is affected by at least five different contexts.

- *Psychological*: who you are and what you bring to the communication; your needs, desires, values and beliefs.
- *Relational*: how we define each other and behave in relation to each other; where power or status lies; whether we like each other (this context can shift while we are communicating).
- *Situational*: the social context within which we are communicating; the rules and conventions that apply in different social conditions (interaction in a classroom or office will differ from interaction in a bar or on a sports field).
- *Environmental*: the physical location; furniture, location, noise level, temperature, season, time of day, and so on.
- *Cultural*: all the learned behaviours and rules that affect the way we communicate; cultural norms; national, ethnic or organisational conventions.

These insights suggest a different model of the communication process. In this model, we are at the centre of two interlocking sets of contexts, seeking to find common ground. Whatever we understand, we have communicated with each other.

Communication succeeds when we increase the area of common understanding (the shaded area in the diagram in Figure 1.3).

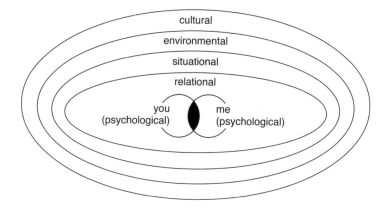

Figure 1.3   A contextual model of communication

We need a new definition of the word 'communication'. And the history of the word itself gives us a clue. 'Communication' derives from the Latin *communis*, meaning 'common', 'shared'. It belongs to the family of words that includes *communion*, *communism* and *community*. When we communicate, we are trying to match meanings.

Or, to put it another way:

> **Communication is the process of creating shared understanding.**

The three levels of understanding

Communication creates understanding on three levels, each underpinning the one above (Figure 1.4).

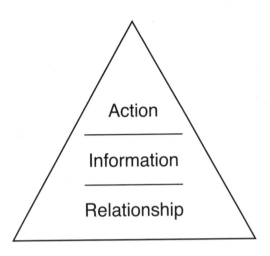

Figure 1.4   The three levels of understanding

As managers, we tend to focus on action as the reason for communicating. Yet, as people, we usually communicate for quite another reason. And here is a vital clue to explain why communication in organisations so often goes wrong.

Relationship: the big issue of small talk

The first and most important reason for communicating is to build relationships with other people. Recent research (commissioned from the Social Issues Research Centre by British Telecom) suggests that about two thirds of our conversation time is entirely devoted to social topics: personal relationships; who is doing what with whom; who is 'in' and who is 'out', and why. There must be a good reason for that.

According to psychologist Robin Dunbar, language evolved as the human equivalent of grooming, the primary means of social bonding among other primates. As social groups among humans became larger (the average human network is about 150, compared to groups of about 50 among other primates), we needed a less time-consuming form of social interaction. We invented language as a way to square the circle. In Dunbar's words: 'language evolved to allow us to gossip' (*Grooming, Gossip and the Evolution of Language*, Faber and Faber, London, 1996).

Gossip is good for us. It tells us where we sit in the social network. And that makes us relax. Physical grooming stimulates production of endorphins – the body's natural painkilling opiates – reducing heart rate and lowering stress. Gossip probably has a similar effect. In fact, the research suggests that gossip is essential to our social, psychological and physical well-being.

We ignore this fundamental quality of conversation at our peril. If we fail to establish a relaxed relationship, everything else in the conversation will become more difficult.

Building rapport

The first task in any conversation is to build rapport. Rapport is the sense that another person is like us. Building rapport is a pattern-matching process. Most rapport-building happens without words: we create rapport through a dance of matching movements, including body orientation, body moves, eye contact, facial expression and tone of voice.

Human beings can create rapport instinctively. Yet these natural dance patterns can disappear in conversations at work; other kinds of relationship sometimes intrude. A little conscious effort to create rapport at the very start of a conversation can make a huge difference to its outcome.

We create rapport through:

- **verbal behaviour;**
- **vocal behaviour; and**
- **physical behaviour.**

Of those three elements, verbal behaviour – the words we use – actually contributes *least* to building rapport.

Overwhelmingly, we believe what we see. In the famous sales phrase, 'the eye buys'. If there is a mismatch between a person's words and their body language, we instantly believe what the body tells us. So building rapport must begin with giving the *physical* signs of being welcoming, relaxed and open.

The music of the voice is the second key factor in establishing rapport. We can vary our *pitch* (how high or low the tone of voice is), *pace* (the speed of speaking) and *volume* (how loudly or softly we speak). Speak quickly and loudly, and raise the pitch of your voice, and you will sound tense or stressed. Create vocal music that is lower in tone, slower and softer, and you will create rapport more easily.

But creating rapport means more than matching body language or vocal tone. We must also match the other person's words, so that they feel we are 'speaking their language'.

Building rapport: a doctor's best practice

Dr Grahame Brown is a medical consultant who wondered why his sessions with patients were so ineffective. He began to realise that the problem was the way he conducted the interview. Getting the relationship right is, he believes, the key to more effective treatment.

My first priority now is to build rapport with the patient in the short time I have with them.

Instead of keeping the head down over the paperwork till a prospective heartsick patient is seated, then greeting them with a tense smile (as all too many doctors do), I now go out into the waiting room to collect patients whenever possible. This gives me the chance to observe in a natural way how they look, how they stand, how they walk and whether they exhibit any 'pain behaviours', such as sighing or limping.

I shake them warmly by the hand and begin a conversation on our way to the consulting area. 'It's warm today, isn't it? Did you find your way here all right? Transport okay?' By the time we are seated, the patient has already agreed with me several times. This has an important effect on our ensuing relationship – we are already allies, not adversaries...

Next, rather than assuming the patient has come to see me about their pain, I ask them what they have come to see me about. Quite often they find this surprising, because they assume that I know all about them from their notes. But even though I will have read their notes, I now assume nothing. I ask open-ended questions that can give me the most information – the facts which are important to them.

(From Griffin, Joe and Tyrrell, Ivan, *Human Givens*, HG Publishing, Brighton, 2004)

For most of us, starting a conversation with someone we don't know is stressful. We can be lost for words. 'Breaking the ice' is a skill many of us would dearly love to develop.

The key is to decrease the tension in the encounter. Look for something in your shared situation to talk about; then ask a question relating to that. The other person must not feel excluded or interrogated, so avoid:

- **talking about yourself; and**
- **asking the other person a direct question about themselves.**

Doing either will *increase* the tension in the conversation. As will doing nothing! So take the initiative. Put them at ease, and you will soon relax yourself.

Learning the art of conversation

1. Copy the other person's body language to create a 'mirror image'.
2. Ask three questions – but no more until you have done the next two things.
3. Find something from what you have just learned that will allow you to compliment the other person – subtly.
4. Find something in what you have found out to agree with.
5. Repeat until the conversation takes on a life of its own.

(With thanks to Chris Dyas)

Information: displaying the shape of our thinking

Once we have created a relaxed relationship, we are ready to share information. So what is information, and how does it operate?

Every time we communicate, information changes shape. Children have enormous fun playing with the way information can alter in the telling. Chinese Whispers and Charades are both games that delightfully exploit our capacity to misunderstand each other.

Understanding – as we've already seen – is mental pattern-matching. 'Ah!' we exclaim when we've understood something, 'I see!' We may have a different *perspective* on a problem from a colleague; we often misunderstand each other because we are approaching the issue from different *angles*. If we disagree with someone, we may say that we *are looking* at it differently. It's all about what patterns we recognise: which patterns match our mental models.

Information is the shape of our thinking. We *create* information inside our heads. Information is never 'out there'; it is always, and only ever, in our minds. And the shape of information constantly changes, evolving, as we think. Information is dynamic.

Information is unique as a resource because of its capacity to generate itself. It's the solar energy of organisation – inexhaustible, with new progeny emerging every time information meets up with itself.

(Margaret J Wheatley, *Leadership and the New Science*, Berrett-Kohler Publishers Inc, San Francisco, 1st edn, 1992)

Creating shared understanding of information, then, means displaying it in a form that the other person can recognise. You could draw pictures or diagrams. Better still, you could find out what mental patterns the other person uses – and then fit your information into them. Pictures and models usually simplify information, making it easier to understand.

When we communicate, we never merely hand over information; we create *meaning* out of that information, and then share that meaning. If the other person can't understand what we mean, then our attempts to communicate have failed.

Action: influencing with our ideas

As well as creating relationships and sharing information, we communicate to promote action. And the key to effective action is not accurate information but persuasive ideas.

Ideas give meaning to information. Put simply, an idea says something about the information. A name is not an idea. These phrases are all names but, for our purposes, they aren't ideas:

- Profit analysis;
- Asian market;
- Operations Director.

To turn them into ideas, we have to create statements about them:

- **Profit analysis shows an upturn in sales of consumables over the last year.**
- **The Asian market has become unstable.**
- **Bill Freeman is now Operations Director.**

These sentences create meaning by saying something about the names. What we have done is very simple: we have created sentences.

> **An idea is a thought expressed as a sentence.**

Ideas are the currency of communication. We are paid for our ideas. When we communicate, we trade ideas. Like currency, ideas come in larger or smaller denominations: there are big ideas, and little ideas. We can assemble the little ones into larger units, by summarising them. Like currencies, ideas have a value and that value can change: some ideas become more valuable as others lose their value. We judge the quality of an idea by how *meaningful* it is.

The most effective communication makes ideas explicit. We may take one idea and pit it against another. We may seek the evidence behind an idea or the consequences pursuing it. We might enrich an idea with our feelings about it. Whatever strategy we adopt, our purpose in communicating is to create and share ideas.

Conversation: the heart of communication

Conversation is the main way we communicate. Through conversation we build relationships, share information and promote our ideas. All the other ways we communicate – interviews, presentations, networking meetings, even written documents – are conversations of some kind. Organisations are networks of conversations.

Conversations are the way we create shared meaning. If we want to improve our communication skills, we could begin by improving our conversations.

2

How conversations work

Conversation is our primary management tool. We converse to
build relationships with colleagues and customers. We influence
others by holding conversations with them. We converse to solve
problems, to co-operate and find new opportunities for action.
Conversation is our way of imagining the future.

It may be good to talk, but conversations at work are often
difficult. A manager summed up the problem to me recently. 'If
we don't re-learn how to talk with each other,' he said, 'frequently
and on a meaningful level, this organisation won't survive.'

What is a conversation?

Conversations are verbal dances. The word derives from the
Latin, 'to move around with'. Like any dance, a conversation has
rules, and standard moves. These allow people to move more
harmoniously together, without stepping on each other's toes or
getting out of step. Different kinds of conversation have different
conventions. Some are implicitly understood; others, for

example in presentations or meetings, must be spelt out in detail and rehearsed.

A conversation is a dynamic of talking and listening. Without the listening, there's no conversation. And the quality of the conversation depends more on the quality of the listening than on the quality of the speaking.

Balancing advocacy and enquiry

Peter Senge, author of *The Fifth Discipline* (Random House Business Books, London, 1993), uses the words 'advocacy' and 'enquiry' to describe talking and listening. Talking is principally the means by which we advocate our point of view, our ideas, our thinking. Listening is the process of enquiring into the other person's point of view, their ideas, their thinking.

Adversarial conversations are pure advocacy. We advocate our own point of view, reasonably and calmly, and become more and more entrenched in our positions.

Advocacy without enquiry simply escalates into conflict. You can see this escalation happening every day. It's exhausting and debilitating. It becomes part of the culture within which managers operate. It can be so upsetting that managers avoid holding conversations at all and retreat behind their office doors – if they are lucky enough to have one.

But conversations that are pure enquiry are also unsatisfactory. If we concentrate solely on listening to the other person, we risk an unclear outcome – or no outcome at all. Indeed, some managers use the skills of enquiry – listening, asking questions, and always looking for the other point of view – as a way of avoiding difficult decisions.

The best conversations balance advocacy and enquiry. They are a rich mix of talking and listening, of stating views and asking questions.

Why do conversations go wrong?

We can all think of conversations at work that have gone wrong. Working out *why* they went wrong may be hard. Conversations are so subtle and they happen so fast. Few of us have been trained in the art of effective conversation. Conversation is a life skill, and – like most life skills – one that we are usually expected to pick up as we go along.

Broadly, there are four main areas where conversations can fail:

- **context;**
- **relationship;**
- **structure;**
- **behaviour.**

These are the four dimensions of conversation. By looking at them, we can begin to understand more clearly how conversations work, why they go wrong, and how we can begin to improve them.

Putting conversations in context

All conversations have a context. They happen for a reason.

Most conversations form part of a larger conversation: they are part of a process or a developing relationship.

Many conversations fail because one or both of us ignore the context. If we don't check that we understand why the conversation is happening, we may very quickly start to misunderstand each other.

The problem may simply be that the conversation never happens. One of the most persistent complaints against managers is that they are not there to talk to: 'I never see him', 'She has no idea what I do', 'He simply refuses to listen'. Other obvious problems that afflict the context of the conversation include:

- **not giving enough time to the conversation;**
- **holding the conversation at the wrong time;**
- **conversing in an uncomfortable, busy or noisy place;**
- **a lack of privacy;**
- **distractions.**

Less obvious, but just as important, are the assumptions that we bring to our conversations. All conversations start from assumptions. If we leave them unquestioned, misunderstandings and conflict can quickly arise. For example, we might assume that:

- **we both know what we are talking about;**
- **we need to agree;**
- **we know how the other person views the situation;**
- **we shouldn't let our feelings show;**
- **the other person is somehow to blame for the problem;**
- **we can be brutally honest;**
- **we need to solve the other person's problem;**
- **we're right and they're wrong.**

These assumptions derive from our opinions about what is true, or about what we – or others – should do. We bring *mental models* to our conversations: constructions about reality that determine how we look at it. For example, I might hold a mental model that we are in business to make a profit; that women have an inherently different management style from men; or that character is determined by some set of national characteristics. Millions of mental models shape and drive our thinking, all the time. We can't think *without* mental models. Thinking is the process of developing and changing our mental models.

All too often, however, conversations become conflicts between these mental models. This is adversarial conversation, and it is one of the most important and deadly reasons why conversations go wrong. (You'll find more about adversarial conversation in Chapter 3.)

Key factors: context

- **Objectives.** Do you both know why you are holding the conversation?
- **Time.** Is this the right time to be holding this conversation? What is the history behind the conversation? Is it part of a larger process?
- **Place.** Are you conversing in a place that is comfortable, quiet and free from distractions?
- **Assumptions.** Do you both understand the assumptions that you are starting from? Do you need to explore them before going further?

Working out the relationship

Our relationship defines the limits and potential of our conversation. We converse differently with complete strangers and with close acquaintances. Conversations are ways of establishing, fixing or changing a relationship.

Relationships are neither fixed nor permanent. They are complex and dynamic. Our relationship operates along a number of dimensions, including:

- **status;**
- **power;**
- **role;**
- **liking.**

All of these factors help to define the territory of the conversation.

Status

We can define status as the rank we grant to another person in relation to us. We normally measure it along a simple (some might say simplistic) scale. We see ourselves simply as higher or lower in status in relation to the other person.

We confer status on others. It's evident in the degree of respect, familiarity or reserve we grant them. We derive our own sense of status from the status we give the other person. We do all this through conversation.

Conversations may fail because the status relationship limits what we say. If we feel low in status relative to the other person, we may agree to everything they say and suppress strongly held ideas of our own. If we feel high in status relative to them, we may tend to discount what they say, put them down, interrupt or ignore them. Indeed, these behaviours are ways of establishing or altering our status in a relationship.

Our status is always at risk. It is created entirely through the other person's perceptions. It can be destroyed or diminished in a moment. Downgrading a person's status can be a powerful way of exerting your authority over them.

Power

Power is the control we can exert over others. If we can influence or control people's behaviour in any way, we have power over them. John French and Bertram Raven (in D Cartwright (ed) *Studies in Social Power*, 1959), identified five kinds of power base:

- *reward power*: **the ability to grant favours for behaviour;**
- *coercive power*: **the ability to punish others;**
- *legitimate power*: **conferred by law or other sets of rules;**

- *referent power*: the 'charisma' that causes others to imitate or idolise;
- *expert power*: deriving from specific levels of knowledge or skill.

Referent power is especially effective. Conversations can become paralysed as one of us becomes overcome by the charisma of the other.
Conversations often fail because they become power struggles. People may seek to exercise different kinds of power at different points in a conversation. If you have little reward power over the other person, for example, you may try to influence them as an expert. If you lack charisma or respect with the other person, you may try to exert authority by appealing to legitimate or to coercive power.

Convening power: an emergent force

People are beginning to talk about a new form of power. Convening power is defined by the Foreign and Commonwealth Office as 'the ability to bring the right people together'. It's the power of 'connectors', who are often at the heart of effective networking. For more, look at Chapter 9.

Role

A role is a set of behaviours that people expect of us. A formal role may be explicitly defined in a job description; an informal role is conferred on us as a result of people's experience of our conversations.
Conversations may fail because our roles are unclear, or in conflict. We tend to converse with each other in role. If the other person knows that your formal role is an accountant, for

example, they will tend to converse with you in that role. If they know that your informal role is usually the devil's advocate, or mediator, or licensed fool, they will adapt their conversation to that role. Seeing people in terms of roles can often lead us to label them with that role. As a result, our conversations can be limited by our mental models about those roles.

Meredith Belbin's team roles

Thousands of managers have now used Belbin's questionnaire to locate themselves among his categories of:

- **chair/co-ordinator;**
- **shaper/team leader;**
- **plant/innovator or creative thinker;**
- **monitor-evaluator/critical thinker;**
- **company worker/implementer;**
- **team worker/team builder;**
- **finisher/detail checker and pusher;**
- **resource investigator/researcher outside the team;**
- **expert.**

The danger is that people may label themselves with a role and start to operate exclusively within it. Our conversations could then be limited by our perceived roles.

'A team is not a bunch of people with job titles, but a congregation of individuals, each of whom has a role that is understood by other members.'
(Meredith Belbin, *Management teams: why they succeed or fail*, Heinemann, 1981)

Liking

Conversations can fail because we dislike each other. But they can also go wrong because we like each other a lot!

The simple distinction between liking and disliking seems crude. We can find people attractive in many different ways or take against them in ways we may not be able – or willing – to articulate. Liking can become an emotional entanglement or even a fully-fledged relationship; dislike can turn a conversation into a vendetta or a curious, half-coded game of tit-for-tat.

These four factors – status, power, role and liking – affect the territorial relationship in the conversation. A successful conversation seeks out the shared territory, the common ground between us. But we guard our own territory carefully. As a result, many conversational rules are about how we ask and give permission for the other person to enter our territory.

The success of a conversation may depend on whether you give or ask clearly for such permission. People often ask for or give permission in code; you may only receive the subtlest hint, or feel inhibited from giving more than a clue of your intentions. Often, it's only when the person reacts that you realise you have intruded on private territory.

Key factors: relationship

- **Status.** Is there a marked difference in status between you? Why is that? How does this difference affect the way you are behaving towards the other person? How do you think it might be affecting their behaviour?
- **Power.** Can you see power being wielded in the conversation? What kind of power and in which direction? How might you both be affecting the power relationship? How do you want to affect it?
- **Role.** What is your role in this conversation? Think about your formal role (your job title perhaps, or contractual position) and your informal role. How do people see you acting in conversations? Can you feel yourself falling naturally into any particular role in the conversation?

- **Liking.** How is the conversation being affected by your feelings towards each other? Is the liking or disliking getting in the way of a productive outcome?
- **Territory.** Where are the boundaries? Are you finding common ground? Where can you give permission for the other person to enter your territory? Where can you ask permission to enter theirs?

Setting a structure

Many of our conversations are a mess. We rush. We wander from point to point. We repeat ourselves. We get stuck in a groove. Some conversations proceed in parallel, with each of us telling our own story or making our own points with no reference to what the other person is saying. If conversation is a verbal dance, we often find ourselves trying to dance two different dances at the same time, or treading on each other's toes.

Why should we worry about the structure of our conversations? After all, conversations are supposed to be living and flexible. Wouldn't a structure make our conversation too rigid and uncomfortable?

Maybe. But all living organisms have structures. They cannot grow and develop healthily unless they conform to fundamental structuring principles.

Conversations, too, have structural principles. The structure of a conversation derives from the way we think. We can think about thinking as a process in two stages (see also Figure 2.1).

First-stage thinking is the thinking we do when we are looking at reality. First-stage thinking allows us to recognise something because it fits into some pre-existing mental pattern or idea. Ideas allow us to make sense of reality. The result of first-stage thinking is that we translate reality into language. We name an object or an event; we turn a complicated physical process into an equation; we simplify a structure by drawing a diagram; we contain a landscape on a map.

Second-stage thinking manipulates the language we have created to achieve a result. Having named something as, say, a cup, we can talk about it coherently. We can judge its effectiveness as a cup, its value to us, how we might use it or improve its design. Having labelled a downturn in sales as a marketing problem, we explore the consequences in marketing terms.

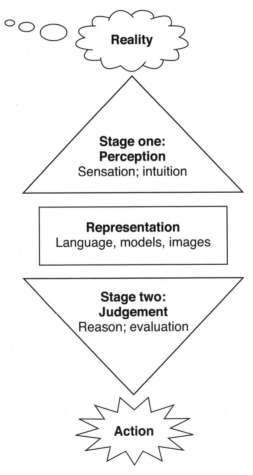

Figure 2.1 The two stages of thinking

Our conversations all follow this simple structure. We cannot talk about anything until we have named it. Conversely, how we name something determines the way we talk about it. The quality of our second-stage thinking depends directly on the quality of our first-stage thinking.

We're very good at second-stage thinking. We have lots of experience in manipulating language. We're so good at it that we can build machines to do it for us: computers are very fast manipulators of binary language.

We aren't nearly so good at first-stage thinking. We mostly give names to things without thinking. The cup is obviously a cup; who would dream of calling it anything else? The marketing problem is obviously a marketing problem – isn't it? As a result, most of our conversations complete the first stage in a few seconds. We leap to judgement.

Suppose we named the cup as – to take a few possibilities at random – a chalice, or a vase, or a trophy. Our second-stage thinking about that object would change radically. Suppose we decided that the marketing problem might be a production problem, a distribution problem, or a personnel problem. We would start to think very differently about it at the second stage.

We prefer to take our perceptions for granted. But no amount of second-stage thinking will make up for faulty or limited first-stage thinking. Good thinking pays attention to both stages. Effective conversations have a first stage and a second stage.

An effective conversation manages structure by:

- **separating the two stages;**
- **checking that we both know what stage we are in;**
- **asking the questions appropriate to each stage.**

Key factors: structure

Each stage of the conversation includes key questions. Use these questions to develop your thinking in each stage.

First-stage thinking

What do we want to achieve?

What are we looking at?

What might it mean?

How else could we look at it?

What else could we call it?

How would someone else see it?

What is it like?

Second-stage thinking

What do we think about this?

How do we evaluate it?

What can we do?

What opportunities are there?

How useful is it?

Why are we interested in this?

How does this fit with our plans?

What shall we do?

Managing behaviour

Conversations are never simply exchanges of words. Supporting the language we use is a whole range of non-verbal communication: the music of our voice, the gestures we use, the way we move our eyes or hold our body, the physical positions we adopt in relation to each other.

We have less control over our non-verbal behaviour than over the way we speak. This may be because we have learnt most of our body language implicitly, by absorbing and imitating the body language of people around us. Our non-verbal communication will sometimes say things to the other person that we don't intend them to know. Under pressure, our bodies leak information. Our feelings come out as gestures.

Conversations often go wrong because we misinterpret non-verbal messages. There are four main reasons for this:

- *Non-verbal messages are ambiguous.* No dictionary can accurately define them. Their meaning can vary according to context, to the degree of intention in giving them, and because they may not consistently reflect feeling.
- *Non-verbal messages are continuous.* We can stop talking but we can't stop behaving! Language is bound by the structures of grammar. Non-verbal communication is not structured in the same way.
- *Non-verbal messages are multi-channel.* Everything is happening at once: eyes, hands, feet, body position. We interpret non-verbal messages holistically, as a whole impression. This makes them strong but unspecific, so that we may not be able to pin down exactly why we get the impression we do.
- *Non-verbal messages are culturally determined.* Research suggests that a few non-verbal messages are universal: everybody seems to smile when they are happy, for example. Most non-verbal behaviours, however, are specific to a culture. A lot of confusion can arise from the misinterpretation of non-verbal messages across a cultural divide.

Effective communicators manage their behaviour. They work hard to align their non-verbal messages with their words. You may feel that trying to manage your own behaviour in the same way is dishonest: 'play-acting' a part that you don't necessarily feel. But we all act when we hold conversations. Managing our behaviour simply means trying to act appropriately.

The most important things to manage are eye contact and body movement. By becoming more conscious of the way you use your eyes and move your limbs, you can reinforce the effect of your words and encourage the other person to contribute more fully to the conversation. Simple actions like keeping your limbs and hands still, or looking steadily at the speaker while they are speaking, can make a big and immediate difference to the quality of the conversation.

Key factors: managing behaviour

- **Check the context.** Don't try to interpret non-verbal messages in isolation from any others, or from the wider situation. Folded arms may mean that someone is hostile to your ideas, or that they are cold.
- **Look for clusters.** If you are picking up a group of non-verbal messages that seem to indicate a single feeling, you may be able to trust your interpretation more fully.
- **Consider past experience.** We can interpret more accurately the behaviour of people we know. We certainly notice changes in their behaviour. We also interpret patterns of behaviour over time more accurately than single instances.
- **Check your perceptions.** Ask questions. You are interpreting observed behaviour, not reading someone's mind. Check out what you observe and make sure that your interpretation is accurate.

3

Seven ways to improve your conversations

Your success as a manager depends on your ability to hold effective and productive conversations. This chapter looks at seven proven strategies to help you improve your conversations.

1. Clarify your objective.
2. Structure your thinking.
3. Manage your time.
4. Find common ground.
5. Move beyond argument.
6. Summarise often.
7. Use visuals.

Don't feel that you must apply all seven at once. Take a single strategy and work at it for a few days. (You should have plenty of conversations to practise on!) Once you feel that you have integrated that skill into your conversations, move on to another.

1. Clarify your objective

Work out at the start of your conversation what you want to achieve.

Think of a conversation as a journey you are taking together. It will very quickly start to wander off track if either of you is unclear where you're going. You will complete the journey effectively only if you both know clearly where you are aiming for.

What's vital is that you *state* your objective clearly at the start. Give a headline. If you know what your main point is, state it at the start of the conversation.

Headlines

Newspapers rely on headlines to get the story's message across quickly. You can do the same in your conversations:

I want to talk to you about...
I've looked at the plan and I've got some suggestions.
I know you're worried about the sales figures. I've got some clues that might help.
I've called this meeting to make a decision about project X.

Of course, you might decide to change your objective in the middle of the conversation – just as you might decide to change direction in the middle of a journey. That's fine, so long as both of you know what you're doing. Too specific an objective at the start might limit your success at the end. This problem is at the heart of negotiation, for example: what would you be willing to settle for, and what is not negotiable?

Objectives roughly divide into two categories:

- **exploring a problem;**
- **finding a solution.**

When you are thinking about your headline, ask 'problem or solution?' You may tend to assume that any conversation about a problem is aiming to find a solution – particularly if the other person has started the conversation. As a result, you may find yourself working towards a solution without accurately defining or understanding the problem. It may be that the other person doesn't want you to offer a solution, but rather to talk through the problem with them.

2. Structure your thinking

You can improve your conversations enormously by giving them structure. The simplest way to structure a conversation is to break it in half.

Thinking, as we have seen can be modelled as a two-stage process. *First-stage thinking* is thinking about a problem; *second-stage thinking* is thinking about a solution.

Many managerial conversations leap to second-stage thinking without spending nearly enough time in the first stage. They look for solutions and almost ignore the problem.

Why this urge to ignore the problem? Perhaps because problems are frightening. To stay with a problem – to explore it, to try to understand it further, to confront it and live with it for a few moments – is too uncomfortable. People don't like living with unresolved problems. Better to deal with it: sort it out; solve it; get rid of it.

Resist the temptation to rush into second-stage thinking. Give the first stage – the problem stage – as much attention and time as you think appropriate. Then give it a little more. And make sure that you are both in the same stage of the conversation at the same time.

Link the stages of your conversation together. Linking helps you to steer the conversation comfortably. Skilled conversation holders can steer the conversation by linking the following:

- **the past and the present;**
- **the problem and the solution;**
- **first-stage and second-stage thinking;**
- **requests and answers;**
- **negative ideas and positive ideas;**
- **opinions about what is true, with speculation about the consequences.**

WASP: welcome; acquire; supply; part

In my early days as a manager, I was introduced to a simple four-stage model of conversation that I still use. It breaks down the two stages of thinking into four steps:

- *Welcome (first-stage thinking).* **At the start of the conversation, state your objectives, set the scene and establish your relationship: 'Why are we talking about this matter? Why** us**?'**
- *Acquire (first-stage thinking).* **The second step is information gathering. Concentrate on finding out as much as possible about the matter, from as many angles as you can. For both of you, listening is vital. You are acquiring knowledge from each other. This part of the conversation should be dominated by questions.**
- *Supply (second-stage thinking).* **Now, at the third step, we summarise what we've learnt and begin to work out what to do with the information. We are beginning to think about how we might move forward: the options that present themselves. It's important at this stage of the conversation to remind yourselves of the objective that you set at the start.**

- *Part (second-stage thinking).* Finally, you work out what you have agreed. You state explicitly the conversation's outcome: the action that will result from it. The essence of the parting stage is that you explicitly agree what is going to happen next. What is going to happen? Who will do it? Is there a deadline? Who is going to check on progress?

From impromptu conversations in the corridor to formal interviews, WASP gives you a simple framework to make sure that the conversation stays on track and results in a practical outcome.

Four types of conversation

This simple four-stage model can become more sophisticated. In this developed model, you hold four conversations, for:

- relationship;
- possibility;
- opportunity;
- action.

These four conversations may form part of a single, larger conversation; they may also take place separately, at different stages of a process or project.

A conversation for relationship ('welcome')

You hold a conversation for relationship to create or develop the relationship you need to achieve your objective. It is an exploration.

A conversation for relationship: key questions

Who are we?
How do we relate to the matter in hand?
What links us?
How do we see things?
What do you see that I can't see?
What do I see that you don't see?
In what ways do we see things similarly, or differently?
How can we understand each other?
Where do we stand?
Can we stand together?

Conversations for relationship are tentative and sometimes awkward. They are often rushed because they can be embarrassing. Think of those tricky conversations you have had with strangers at parties: they are good examples of conversations for relationship. A managerial conversation for relationship should move beyond the 'What do you do? Where do you live?' questions. You are defining your relationship to each other, and to the matter in hand.

A conversation for possibility ('acquire')

A conversation for possibility continues the exploration: it develops first-stage thinking. It asks what you *might* be looking at.

A conversation for possibility is *not* about whether to do something, or what to do. It seeks to find new ways of looking at the problem.

There are a number of ways of doing this.

- **Look at it from a new angle.**
- **Ask for different interpretations of what's happening.**

- Try to distinguish what you're looking at from what you think about it.
- Ask how other people might see it.
- Break the problem into parts.
- Isolate one part of the problem and look at it in detail.
- Connect the problem into a wider network of ideas.
- Ask what the problem is like. What does it look like, or feel like?

Conversations for possibility are potentially a source of creativity: brainstorming is a good example. But they can also be uncomfortable: exploring different points of view may create conflict.

A conversation for possibility: key questions

What's the problem?
What are we trying to do?
What's the real problem?
What are we really trying to do?
Is this a problem?
How could we look at this from a different angle?
Can we interpret this differently?
How could we do this?
What does it look like from another person's point of view?
What makes this different from last time?
Have we ever done anything like this before?
Can we make this simpler?
Can we look at this in bits?
What is this like?
What does this feel or look like?

Manage this conversation with care. Make it clear that this is not decision time. Encourage the other person to give you ideas. Take care not to judge or criticise. Do challenge or probe what the other person says. In particular, manage the emotional content of this conversation with care. Acknowledge people's feelings and look for the evidence that supports them.

A conversation for opportunity ('supply')

A conversation for opportunity takes us into second-stage thinking. This is fundamentally a conversation about planning. Many good ideas never become reality because people don't map out paths of opportunity. A conversation for opportunity is designed to construct such a path. You are choosing what to do. You assess what you would need to make action possible: resources, support and skills. This conversation is more focused than a conversation for possibility: in choosing from among a number of possibilities, you are finding a sense of common purpose.

A conversation for opportunity: key questions

Where can we act?
What could we do?
Which possibilities do we build on?
Which possibilities are feasible?
What target do we set ourselves?
Where are the potential obstacles?
How will we know that we've succeeded?

The bridge from possibility to opportunity is *measurement*. This is where you begin to set targets, milestones, obstacles, measures of success. How will you be able to judge when you have achieved an objective?

Recall your original objective. Has it changed? Conversations for opportunity can become more exciting by placing yourselves in a future where you have achieved your objective. What does such a future look and feel like? What is happening in this future? How can you plan your way towards it? Most people plan by starting from where they are and extrapolate current actions towards a desired objective. By 'backward planning' from an imagined future, you can find new opportunities for action.

A conversation for action ('part')

This is where you agree what to do, who will do it and when it will happen. Translating opportunity into action needs more than agreement; you need to generate a promise, a commitment to act.

Managers often remark that getting action is one of the hardest aspects of managing people. 'Have you noticed', one senior director said to me recently, 'how people seem never to do what they've agreed to do?' Following up on agreed actions can become a major time-waster. A conversation for action is the first step in solving this problem. It's vital that the promise resulting from a conversation for action is recorded.

A conversation for action: key stages

A conversation for action is a dynamic between asking and promising. It takes a specific form:

- You ask the other person to do something by a certain time. Make it clear that this is a request, not an order. Orders may get immediate results, but they rarely generate commitment.
- The other person has four possible answers to this request:
  - They can accept.
  - They can decline.

- They may commit to accepting or declining at a later date ('I'll let you know by x').
- They can make a counter-offer ('I can't do that, but I can do x').
- The conversation results in a promise ('I will do x for you by time y').

This four-stage model of conversation – either in its simple WASP form, or in the more sophisticated form of relationship–possibility–opportunity–action – will serve you well in the wide range of conversations you will hold as a manager. Some of your conversations will include all four stages; some will concentrate on one more than another.

These conversations will only be truly effective if you hold them *in order*. The success of each conversation depends on the success of the conversation before it. If you fail to resolve a conversation, it will continue underneath the next *in code*. Unresolved aspects of a conversation for relationship, for instance, can become conflicts of possibility, hidden agendas or 'personality clashes'. Possibilities left unexplored become lost opportunities. And promises to act that have no real commitment behind them will create problems later.

3. Manage your time

Conversations take time, and time is the one entirely non-renewable resource. It's vital that you manage time well, both for and in your conversations.

Managing time for the conversation

Work out how much time you have. Don't just assume that there is no time. Be realistic. If necessary, make an appointment at another time to hold the conversation. Make sure it's a time that both of you find convenient.

Managing time in the conversation

Most conversations proceed at a varying rate. Generally, an effective conversation will probably start quite slowly and get faster as it goes on. But there are no real rules about this.

You know that a conversation is going too fast when people interrupt each other a lot, when parallel conversations start, when people stop listening to each other and when people start to show signs of becoming uncomfortable.

Conversations can go too fast because:

- we become solution-oriented;
- feelings take over;
- we succumb to 'groupthink' (everybody starts thinking alike to reinforce the group);
- we're enjoying ourselves too much;
- assumptions go unchallenged;
- people stop asking questions;
- arguments flare up.

Conversely, you know that a conversation is slowing down when one person starts to dominate the conversation, when questions dry up, when people pause a lot, when the energy level in the conversation starts to drop or when people show signs of weariness.

Conversations may go too slowly because:

- the conversation becomes problem-centred;
- too much analysis is going on;
- people talk more about the past than the future;
- more and more questions are asked;
- people start to repeat themselves;
- the conversation wanders;
- people hesitate before saying anything.

Try to become aware of how fast the conversation is proceeding, and how fast you think it *should* be going. Here are some simple tactics to help you regain control of time in your conversations.

To slow down a conversation

- Reflect what the other person says rather than replying directly to it.
- Summarise their remark before moving on to your own.
- Go back a stage in the conversation.
- Ask open questions: questions that can't be answered 'yes' or 'no'.
- Pause. Take a break.
- Use the Ladder of Inference. (See below.)

To speed up a conversation:

- Push for action. 'What shall we *do*?' 'What do you propose?'

- Summarise and close one stage of the conversation.
- Look for the implications of what the other person is saying. 'What does that mean in terms of...?' 'How does this affect our plans?' 'So what action is possible here?'
- Ask for new ideas and offer some new ones of your own.

Speeding up is probably a more common cause of conversation failure than slowing down. Try to slow the conversation down consciously and give first-stage thinking a reasonable amount of time to happen. This technique is an integral part of the skills of enquiry, which we explore further in Chapter 4.

4. Find common ground

Conversations are ways of finding common ground. You mostly begin in your own private territory, then use the conversation to find boundaries and the openings where you can cross over to the other person's ground.

Notice how you ask for, and give, permission for these moves to happen. If you are asking permission to move into new territory, you might:

- **make a remark tentatively;**
- **express yourself with lots of hesitant padding: 'perhaps we might...', 'I suppose I think...', 'It's possible that...';**
- **pause before speaking;**
- **look away or down a lot;**
- **explicitly ask permission: 'Do you mind if I mention...?' 'May I speak freely about...?'.**

You do not proceed until the other person has given their permission. Such permission may be explicit: 'Please say what you like'; 'I would really welcome your honest opinion'; 'I don't mind you talking about that'. Other signs of permission might be in the person's body language or behaviour: nodding, smiling, leaning forward.

Conversely, refusing permission can be explicit – 'I'd rather we didn't talk about this' – or in code. The person may evade your question, wrap up an answer in clouds of mystification or reply with another question. Their non-verbal behaviour is more likely to give you a hint of their real feelings: folding their arms, sitting back in the chair, becoming restless, evading eye contact.

5. Move beyond argument

One of the most effective ways of improving your conversations is to develop them beyond argument.

Most people are better at talking than at listening. At school, we often learn the skills of *debate*: of taking a position, holding it, defending it, convincing others of its worth and attacking any position that threatens it.

As a result, conversations have a habit of becoming *adversarial*. Instead of searching out the common ground, people hold their own corner and treat every move by the other person as an attack. Adversarial conversations set up a boxing match between competing opinions.

Opinions are ideas gone cold. They are assumptions about what should be true, rather than conclusions about what is true in specific circumstances. Opinions might include:

- **stories (about what happened, what may have happened, why it happened);**
- **explanations (of why something went wrong, why it failed);**
- **justifications for doing what was done;**
- **gossip (perhaps to make someone feel better at the expense of others);**
- **generalisations (to save the bother of thinking);**
- **wrong-making (to establish power over the other person).**

Opinions are often mistaken for the truth. Whenever you hear someone – maybe yourself – saying that something is 'a well-established fact', you can be certain that they are voicing an opinion. Adversarial conversation stops the truth from emerging. Arguing actually stops you exploring and discovering ideas. And the quality of the conversation rapidly worsens: people are too busy defending themselves, too frightened and too battle-fatigued to do any better.

The Ladder of Inference

The Ladder of Inference is a powerful model that helps you move beyond argument. It was developed initially by Chris Argyris (see *The Fifth Discipline Handbook*, edited by Peter Senge et al, Nicholas Brealey, London, 1994). He pictures the way people think in conversations as a ladder. At the bottom of the ladder is observation; at the top, action.

- **From your observation, you step on to the first rung of the ladder by selecting *data*. (You choose what to look at.)**
- **On the second rung, you infer *meaning* from your experience of similar data.**
- **On the third rung, you generalise those meanings into *assumptions*.**
- **On the fourth rung, you construct mental models (or *beliefs*) out of those assumptions.**
- **You act on the basis of your mental models.**

You travel up and down this ladder whenever you hold a conversation. You are much better at climbing up than stepping down. In fact, you can leap up all the rungs in a few seconds. These 'leaps of abstraction' allow you to act more quickly, but they can also limit the course of the conversation. Even more worryingly, your mental models help you to select data from future observation, further limiting the range of the conversation. This is a 'reflexive loop'; you might call it a mindset.

The Ladder of Inference gives you more choices about where to go in a conversation. It helps you to slow down your thinking. It allows you to:

- **become more aware of your own thinking;**
- **make that thinking available to the other person;**
- **ask them about their thinking.**

Above all, it allows you to defuse an adversarial conversation by 'climbing down' from private beliefs, assumptions and opinions, and then 'climbing up' to shared meanings and beliefs.

The key to using the Ladder of Inference is to ask questions. This helps you to find the differences in the way people think, what they have in common and how they might reach shared understanding.

- **What's the data that underlies what you've said?**
- **Do we agree on the data?**
- **Do we agree on what they mean?**
- **Can you take me through your reasoning?**
- **When you say [what you've said], do you mean [my rewording of it]?**

For example, if someone suggests a particular course of action, you can carefully climb down the ladder by asking:

- **'Why do you think this might work?' 'What makes this a good plan?'**
- **'What assumptions do you think you might be making?' 'Have you considered...?'**
- **'How would this affect...?' 'Does this mean that...?'**
- **'Can you give me an example?' 'What led you to look at this in particular?'**

Even more powerfully, the Ladder of Inference can help you to offer your own thinking for the other person to examine. If you are suggesting a plan of action, you can ask:

- **'Can you see any flaws in my thinking?'**
- **'Would you look at this stuff differently?'** 'How would you put this together?'**
- **'Would this look different in different circumstances?'** 'Are my assumptions valid?'**
- **'Have I missed anything?'**

The beauty of this model is that you need no special training to use it. Neither does the other participant in the conversation. You can use it immediately, as a practical way to intervene in conversations that are collapsing into argument.

6. Summarise often

Perhaps the most important of all the skills of conversation is the skill of summarising. Summaries:

- **allow you to state your objective, return to it and check that you have achieved it;**
- **help you to structure your thinking;**
- **help you to manage time more effectively;**
- **help you to seek the common ground between you;**
- **help you to move beyond adversarial thinking.**

Simple summaries are useful at key turning points in a conversation. At the start, summarise your most important point or your objective. As you want to move on from one stage to the next, summarise where you think you have both got to and check that the other person agrees with you. At the end of the conversation, summarise what you have achieved and the action steps you both need to take.

To summarise means to reinterpret the other person's ideas in your own language. It involves *recognising* the specific point they've made, *appreciating* the position from which they say it and *understanding* the beliefs that inform that position. Recognising what someone says doesn't imply that you agree with it. Rather, it implies that you have taken the point into account. Appreciating the other person's feelings on the matter doesn't mean that you feel the same way, but it does show that you respect those feelings. And understanding the belief may not mean that you share it, but it does mean that you consider it important. Shared problem solving becomes much easier if those three basic summarising tactics come into play.

Of course, summaries must be genuine. They must be supported by all the non-verbal cues that demonstrate your recognition, appreciation and understanding. And those cues will look more genuine if you actually recognise, appreciate and – at least seek to – understand.

7. Use visuals

It's said that people remember about 20 per cent of what they hear, and over 80 per cent of what they see. If communication is the process of making your thinking visible, your conversations will certainly benefit from some way of being able to see your ideas.

There are lots of ways in which you can achieve a visual image of your conversation. The obvious ways include scribbling on the nearest bit of paper or using a flip chart. Less obvious visual aids include the gestures and facial expressions you make. Less obvious still – but possibly the most powerful – are word pictures: the images people can create in each other's minds with the words they use.

Recording your ideas on paper

In my experience, conversations nearly always benefit from being recorded visually. The patterns and pictures and diagrams and doodles that you scribble on a pad help you to listen, to summarise and to keep track of what you've covered. More creatively, they become the focus for the conversation: in making the shape of your thinking visible on the page, you can ensure that you are indeed sharing understanding.

Recording ideas in this way – on a pad or a flip chart – also helps to make conversations more democratic. Once on paper, ideas become common property: all parties to the conversation can see them, add to them, comment on them and combine them.

What is really needed, of course, is a technique that is flexible enough to follow the conversation wherever it might go: a technique that can accommodate diverse ideas while maintaining your focus on a clear objective. If the technique could actually help you to develop new ideas, so much the better.

Fortunately, such a technique exists. It's called mindmapping. Mindmaps are powerful first-stage thinking tools. By emphasising the links between ideas, they encourage you to think more creatively and efficiently.

Mindmaps

Mindmaps are powerful first-stage thinking tools. By emphasising the links between ideas, they encourage us to think more creatively and efficiently.

To make a mindmap:

- Put a visual image of your subject in the centre of a plain piece of paper.
- Write down anything that comes to mind that connects to the central idea.

- Write single words, in BLOCK CAPITALS, along lines radiating from the centre.
- Main ideas will tend to gravitate to the centre of the map; details will radiate towards the edge.
- Every line must connect to at least one other line.
- Use visual display: colour, pattern, highlights.
- Identify the groups of ideas that you have created. **Try to have no more than six.** Give each a heading and put the groups into a number order. .

Mindmaps are incredibly versatile conversational tools. They can help you in any situation where you need to record, assemble, organise or generate ideas. They force you to listen attentively, so that you can make meaningful connections; they help you to concentrate on what you are saying, rather than writing; and they store complicated information on one sheet of paper.

Try out mindmaps in relatively simple conversations to begin with. Record a phone conversation using a mindmap and see how well you get on with the technique. Extend your practice to face-to-face conversations and invite the other person to look at and contribute to the map.

A variation on mindmaps is to use sticky notes to record ideas. By placing one idea on each note, you can assemble the notes on a wall or tabletop and move them around to find logical connections or associations between them. This technique is particularly useful in brainstorming sessions or conversations that are seeking to solve complex problems.

Using metaphors

Metaphors are images of ideas in concrete form. The word means 'transferring' or 'carrying over'. A metaphor carries your meaning from one thing to another. It enables your listener to see something in a new way, by picturing it as something else.

Metaphors use the imagination to support and develop your ideas.

Metaphors bring your meaning alive in the listener's mind. They shift the listener's focus and direct their attention to what the speaker wants them to see. They stir their feelings. Metaphors can build your commitment to another person's ideas and help you to remember them.

If you want to find a metaphor to make your thinking more creative and your conversation more interesting, you might start by simply listening out for them in the conversation you are holding. You will find you use many metaphors without even noticing them. If you are still looking, you might try asking yourself some simple questions:

- **What's the problem like?**
- **If this were a different situation – a game of cricket, a medieval castle, a mission to Mars, a kindergarten – how would I deal with it?**
- **How would a different kind of person manage the issue: a gardener, a politician, an engineer, a hairdresser, an actor?**
- **What does this situation feel like?**
- **If this problem were an animal, what species of animal would it be?**
- **How could I describe what's going on as if it were in the human body?**

Explore your answers to these questions and develop the images that spring to mind. You need to be in a calm, receptive frame of mind to do this: the conversation needs to slow down and reflect on its own progress. Finding metaphors is very much first-stage thinking, because metaphors are tools to help you see reality in new ways.

You will know when you've hit on a productive metaphor. The conversation will suddenly catch fire (that's a metaphor!). You will feel a sudden injection of energy and excitement as you realise that you are thinking in a completely new way.

4

The skills of enquiry

The skills of enquiry are the skills of listening. And the quality of your conversation depends on the quality of your listening.

Only by enquiring into the other person's ideas can you respond honestly and fully to them. Only by discovering the mental models and beliefs that underlie those ideas can you explore the landscape of their thinking. Only by finding out how they think can you begin to persuade them to your way of thinking.

Skilled enquiry actually helps the other person to think better. Listening – real, deep, attentive listening – can liberate their thinking.

I've summarised the skills of enquiry under seven headings:

- **paying attention;**
- **treating the speaker as an equal;**
- **cultivating ease;**
- **encouraging;**
- **asking quality questions;**
- **rationing information;**
- **giving positive feedback.**

Acquiring these skills will help you to give the other person the respect and space they deserve to develop their own ideas – to make their thinking visible.

Paying attention

Paying attention means concentrating on what the other person is saying. That sounds simple: how can we listen without paying attention?

Of course, this is what happens most of the time. We think we're listening, but we aren't. We finish the other person's sentences. We interrupt. We moan, sigh, grunt, laugh or cough. We fill pauses with our own thoughts, stories or theories. We look at our watch or around the room. We think about the next meeting, or the next report, or the next meal. We frown, tap our fingers, destroy paperclips and glance at our diary. We give advice. We give more advice.

We think our own thoughts when we should be silencing them. Real listening means shutting down our own thinking and allowing the other person's thinking to enter.

A lot of what we hear when we listen to another person is our effect on them. If we are paying proper attention, they will become more intelligent and articulate. Poor attention will make them hesitate, stumble and doubt the soundness of their thinking. Poor attention makes people more stupid.

I think that, deep down, we have two mental models about listening. We hold them so deeply that we're hardly aware of them. And they do more to damage the quality of our listening than anything else.

The first mental model is that *people listen in order to work out a reply*. This seems a reasonable enough idea. But it's wrong. If people listen so that they can work out what *they* should think, then they aren't listening closely enough to what *the other person* thinks. They are not paying attention.

The second mental model *is that people reply in order to tell the other person what to think.* In fact, this model implies that people will talk to us only because they *want* our ideas. This model, too, is wrong.

Listening well means helping the other person to find out their ideas. The mind containing the problem probably also contains the solution. Their solution is likely to be much better than ours *because it's theirs.* Paying attention means helping the other person to make their thinking visible.

Of course, the other person may actually want advice. But don't assume that this is the case. Wait for them to ask; if necessary, ask them what they want from you. Don't rush. Give them the chance to find their own ideas first. Paying attention in this way will probably slow the conversation down more than you feel is comfortable. Adjust your own tempo to that of the other person. Wait longer than you want to.

Listen. Listen. And then listen some more. And when they can't think of anything else to say, ask: 'What else do you think about this? What else can you think of? What else comes to mind?' That invitation to talk more can bring even the weariest brain back to life.

Interrupting

Interrupting is the most obvious symptom of poor attention. It's irresistible. Some demon inside us seems to compel us to fill the other person's pauses with words. It's as if the very idea of silence is terrifying.

Mostly people interrupt because they are making assumptions. Here are a few. Next time you interrupt someone in a conversation, ask yourself which of them you are applying.

- **My idea is better than theirs.**
- **The answer is more important than the problem.**
- **I have to utter my idea fast and if I don't interrupt, I'll lose my chance (or forget it).**
- **I know what they're going to say.**

- They don't need to finish the sentence because my rewrite is an improvement.
- They can't improve this idea any further, so I might as well improve it for them.
- I'm more important than they are.
- It's more important for me to be seen to have a good idea than for me to let them finish.
- Interrupting will save time.

Put like that, these assumptions are shown up for what they are: presumptuous, arrogant, silly. You're usually wrong when you assume that you know what the other person is about to say. If you allow them to continue, they will often come up with something more interesting, more colourful and more personal.

Allowing quiet

Once you stop interrupting, the conversation will become quieter. Pauses will appear. The other person will stop talking and you won't fill the silence.

These pauses are like junctions. The conversation has come to a crossroads. You have a number of choices about where you might go next. Either of you might make that choice. If you are interested in persuading, you will seize the opportunity and make the choice yourself. But, if you are enquiring, then you give the speaker the privilege of making the choice.

There are two kinds of pause. One is a filled pause; the other is empty. Learn to distinguish between the two.

Some pauses are filled with thought. Sometimes, the speaker will stop. They will go quiet, perhaps suddenly. They will look elsewhere, probably into a longer distance. They are busy on an excursion. You're not invited. But they will want you to be there at the crossroads when they come back. You are privileged that they have trusted you to wait. So wait.

The other kind of pause is an empty one. Nothing much is happening. The speaker doesn't stop suddenly; instead, they seem to fade away. You are standing at the crossroads in the conversation together, and neither of you is moving. The energy seems to drop out of the conversation. The speaker's eyes don't focus anywhere. If they are comfortable in your company, they may focus on you as a cue for you to choose what move to make.

Wait out the pause. If the pause is empty, the speaker will probably say so in a few moments. 'I can't think of anything else.' 'That's it, really.' 'So. There we are. I'm stuck now.' Try asking that question: 'Can you think of anything else?' Resist the temptation to move the conversation on by asking a more specific question. The moment you do that, you have closed down every other possible journey that you might take together: you are dictating the road to travel. Make sure that you only do so once the other person is ready to let you take the lead.

Showing that you are paying attention

Your face will show the other person whether you are paying attention to them. In particular, your eyes will speak volumes about the quality of your listening.

By behaving *as if* you are interested, you can sometimes *become* more interested.

How to show that you are paying attention

Pay attention! If you actually pay attention, you will look as if you are paying attention.

Relax your facial muscles. Try not to frown. No rigid smiles.

Keep your eyes on the person doing the talking. If you take your eyes away from them, be ready to bring your gaze back to them soon. (The speaker will probably look away frequently: that's what we do when we're thinking.)

> **Think about the angle at which you are sitting or
> standing.** Sixty degrees gives eyes a useful escape lane.
> **Use minimal encouragers.** (For more, look below under
> 'Encouraging'.)
> **Make notes.** If necessary, ask them to pause while you
> make your note.

It may be that such attentive looking actually inhibits the
speaker. In some cultures, looking equates to staring and is a sign
of disrespect. You need to be sensitive to these possible
individual or cultural distinctions and adapt your eye
movements accordingly. Generally, people do not look nearly
enough at those they are listening to. The person speaking will
pick up the quality of your attention through your eyes – possibly
unconsciously – and the quality of their thinking will improve as
a result.

Treating the speaker as an equal

You will only be able to enquire well if you treat the speaker as an
equal. The moment you make your relationship unequal,
confusion will result. If you place yourself higher than them in
status, you will discourage them from thinking well. If you place
them higher than you, you will start to allow your own
inhibitions to disrupt your attention to what they are saying.

Patronising the speaker is the greatest enemy of equality in
conversations. This conversational sin derives from the way
people are treated as children – and the way some people
subsequently treat children. Sometimes children have to be
treated like children. It is necessary to:

- **decide for them;**
- **direct them;**

- **tell them what to do;**
- **assume that adults know better than they do;**
- **worry about them;**
- **take care of them;**
- **control them;**
- **think for them.**

There is a tendency to carry this patronising behaviour over into conversations with other adults. As soon as you think you know better than the other person, or provide the answers for them, or suggest that their thinking is inadequate, you are patronising them. You can't patronise somebody and pay them close attention at the same time.

Treat the other person as an equal and you won't be able to patronise them. If you don't value somebody's ideas, don't hold conversations with them. But if you want ideas that are better than your own, if you want better outcomes and improved working relationships, work hard on giving other people the respect that they and their ideas deserve.

Cultivating ease

Good thinking happens in a relaxed environment. Cultivating ease will allow you to enquire more deeply, and discover more ideas.

Most people aren't used to ease and may actually argue against it. They're so used to urgency that they can't imagine working in any other way. Many organisations actually dispel ease from the workplace. Ease is equated with sloth. If you're not working flat out, chased by deadlines and juggling 50 assignments at the same time, you're not worth your salary. It's assumed that the best thinking happens in such a climate.

This is wrong. Urgency keeps people from thinking well. They're too busy doing. After all, doing is what gets results, isn't it? Not when people have to think to get them. Sometimes, the best results only appear by *not* doing: by paying attention to someone else's ideas with a mind that is alert, comfortable, and at ease. When you are at ease, the solution to a problem will appear as if by magic.

How to cultivate ease

Find the time. If the situation is urgent, postpone the conversation.
Make space. A quiet space; a neutral space; a comfortable space.
Banish distractions. Unplug the phones. Leave the building. Barricade the door.

Cultivating ease in a conversation is largely a behavioural skill. Make yourself comfortable. Lean back, breathe out, smile, look keen, and slow down your speaking rhythm.

Encouraging

In order to liberate the other person's ideas, you may need to do more than pay attention, treat them as an equal and cultivate ease. You may need to actively encourage them to give you their ideas.

Remember that the other person's thinking is to a large extent the result of the effect you have on them. So if you:

- **suggest that they change the subject;**
- **try to convince them of your point of view before listening to their point of view;**
- **reply tit-for-tat to their remarks; or**
- **encourage them to compete with you,**

– you aren't encouraging them to develop their thinking. You're not enquiring properly.

Competitiveness is one of the worst enemies of encouragement. It's easy to slip into a ritual of using the speaker's ideas to promote your own. It's all part of the tradition of adversarial thinking that is so highly valued in Western society.

If the speaker feels that you are competing with them in the conversation, they will limit not only what they say but also what they think. Competition forces people to think only those thoughts that will help them win. Similarly, if you feel that the speaker is trying to compete with you, don't allow yourself to enter the competition. This is much harder to achieve. The Ladder of Inference (see Chapter 3) is one very powerful tool that will help you to defuse competitiveness in your conversations.

Instead of competing, welcome the difference in your points of view. Encourage a positive acknowledgement that you see things differently and that you must deal with that difference if the conversation is to move forward.

Minimal encouragers

Minimal encouragers are brief, supportive statements and actions that convey attention and understanding.
   They can be:

- sub-vocalisations: 'uh-huh', 'mm';
- words and phrases: 'right', 'really?', 'I see';
- repeating key words.

Behaviours can include:

- leaning forward;
- focusing eye contact;
- head-nodding.

Benefits:

- can support the speaker without interrupting them;
- demonstrate your interest;
- encourage the speaker to continue;
- show appreciation of particular points: successes, ideas the speaker finds important;
- indicate recognition of emotion or deep feeling.

Potential problems:

- can be used to direct the course of the conversation: a subtle form of influence;
- can reinforce the speaker's behaviour in a particular direction: they may start to say things in the hope of receiving the 'prize' of a minimal encourager;
- if unsynchronised with other behaviours, may indicate impatience or a desire to move on;
- can become a ritualised habit, empty of meaning.

Asking quality questions

Questions are the most obvious way to enquire into other people's thinking. Yet it's astonishing how rarely managers ask quality questions.

Questions, of course, can be loaded with assumptions. They can be politically charged. In some conversations, the most important questions are never asked because to do so would be to challenge the centre of authority. To ask a question can sometimes seem like revealing an unacceptable ignorance. In some organisations, to ask them is simply 'not done'. 'Questioning,' said Samuel Johnson on one occasion, 'is not the mode of conversation among gentlemen.'

Questions can also be used in ways that don't promote enquiry. Specifically, managers sometimes use questions to:

- **emphasise the difference between their ideas and other people's;**
- **ridicule or make the other person look foolish;**
- **criticise in disguise;**
- **find fault;**
- **make themselves look clever;**
- **express a point of view in code;**
- **force the other person into a corner;**
- **create an argument.**

The only legitimate use of a question is to foster enquiry. Questions help you to:

- **find out facts;**
- **check your understanding;**
- **help the other person to improve their understanding;**
- **invite the other person to examine your own thinking;**
- **request action.**

The best questions open up the other person's thinking. A question that helps the other person think further, develop an idea or make their thoughts more visible to you both, is a high-quality question.

A whole repertoire of questions is available to help you enquire more fully. Specifically, we can use six types of questions:

- *Closed questions.* **Can only be answered 'yes' or 'no'.**
- *Leading questions.* **Put the answer into the other person's mouth.**
- *Controlling questions.* **Help you to take the lead in the conversation.**
- *Probing questions.* **Build on an earlier question, or dig deeper.**

- *Open questions*. Cannot be answered 'yes' or 'no'.
- *Reflecting questions*. Restate the last remark with no new request.

Remember also the Ladder of Inference from Chapter 3. This powerful tool can provide questions that allow you to enquire into the speaker's thinking. You can also use it to invite them to enquire into yours.

The highest quality questions actually liberate the other person's thinking. They remove the assumptions that block thinking and replace them with other assumptions that set it free. The key is identifying the assumption that might be limiting the other person's thinking. You don't have to guess aright: asking the question may tell you whether you've identified it correctly; if it doesn't, it may well open up the speaker's thinking anyway.

These high quality questions are broadly 'What if' questions. You can either ask a question in the form 'What if this assumption weren't true?' or in the form 'What if the opposite assumption were true?'

Examples of the first kind of question might include:

- **What if you became chief executive tomorrow?**
- **What if I weren't your manager?**
- **What if you weren't limited in your use of equipment?**

Examples of the second kind might include:

- **What if you weren't limited by a budget?**
- **What if customers were actually flocking to us?**
- **What if you knew that you were vital to the company's success?**

People are often inhibited from developing their thinking by two deep assumptions. One is that they are incapable of thinking well about something, or achieving something. The other is that they don't deserve to think well or achieve. Asking good questions can help you to encourage the other person to overcome these inhibitors and grow as a competent thinker.

Rationing information

Information is power. Sometimes, as part of enquiry, you can supply information that will empower the speaker to think better. Withholding information is an abuse of your power over them.

The difficulty is that giving information disrupts the dynamic of listening and enquiring. A few simple guidelines will help you to ration the information that you supply.

- *Don't interrupt.* **Let the speaker finish before giving any new information. Don't force information into the middle of their sentence.**
- *Time your intervention.* **Ask yourself when the most appropriate time might be to offer the information.**
- *Filter the information.* **Only offer information that you think will improve the speaker's thinking. Resist the temptation to amplify some piece of information that is not central to the direction of their thinking.**
- *Don't give information to show off.* **You may be tempted to give information to demonstrate how expert or up to date you are. Resist that temptation.**

Asking the speaker for information is also something you should ration carefully. You need to make that request at the right time, and for the right reason. To ask for it at the wrong time may close down their thinking and deny you a whole area of valuable ideas.

Following this advice may mean that you have to listen without fully understanding what the speaker is saying. You may even completely misunderstand for a while. Remember that enquiry is about helping the other person clarify their thinking. If asking for information will help only you – and not the speaker

– you should consider delaying your request. In enquiry, it's more important to let the speaker do their thinking than to understand fully what they are saying. This may seem strange, but if you let the speaker work out their thinking rather than keeping you fully informed, they will probably be better able to summarise their ideas clearly to you when they've finished.

Giving positive feedback

Feedback is the way we check that our enquiry has been successful. But feedback can do more. It can prepare us to switch the mode of conversation from enquiry to persuasion. It can also help us to end a conversation; summarising your response to what the speaker has said and providing the foundations for a conversation for action.

There are two kinds of feedback: positive and negative. It's obvious in simple terms how they differ. Positive feedback is saying that we like, appreciate and value the speaker's ideas. Negative feedback is saying that we dislike them, are hostile to them or place no value on them.

Clearly the two kinds of feedback have wider implications. Positive feedback encourages the other person to go on thinking. Negative feedback is likely to stop them thinking at all. Positive feedback also encourages the speaker to value their own thinking; negative feedback tells them that their thinking is worthless. Positive feedback makes people more intelligent. Negative feedback makes them more stupid.

Negative feedback is usually a sign that we are adopting what one consultant calls 'Negative reality norm theory'. This is the theory that only negative attitudes are realistic. We see this theory at work every day in our newspapers. News, almost by definition, is bad news. The phrase 'good news' is virtually a contradiction in terms.

We live out the theory in our everyday lives and in our conversations. To be positive is to be naive and simplistic; it makes us vulnerable. To be negative is to be well informed and protected from the 'slings and arrows of outrageous fortune'. Whenever we say 'we must be realistic', we usually mean that we should emphasise the negative aspects of the situation.

Given this social norm, to be positive can seem like challenging reality, or importing some new and alien idea into our picture of it. Actually, of course, the positive is merely another part of our picture of reality. In adding it to the negative, we are completing the picture, not distorting it.

The best kind of feedback is *genuine, succinct* and *specific*. If you fake it, they will rumble you. If you go on, they will suspect your honesty. If you are too general, they will find it hard to make use of the feedback.

Balancing appreciation and criticism

We tend to think of feedback as a one-off activity. Actually, we are feeding back to the speaker all the time we are listening to them. Be sure that the continuous feedback you give indicates your respect for them, as people and as thinkers, even if you disagree with their ideas.

Make sure that your positive feedback outweighs the negative. A good working ratio might be five-to-one: five positive remarks for every negative one. This can sometimes be difficult to achieve! The speaker may not have delivered any very good ideas. It's more likely that you can only see what's bad, or wrong, or incomplete, or inaccurate, about their ideas. Years of training and experience in critical thinking may have taught you not to comment on what you approve or like.

Look for things to be positive about. I think that this is a basic managerial skill, as well as a conversational one. Praise – genuine, succinct and specific – does more to help you manage than any other activity, because it helps people to think and work better than any other motivator.

Get into the habit of asking: 'What's good about what this person is saying?' Force yourself, if necessary, to find some answers to that question; then be sure to give those answers to the speaker. It's easier to ask this question if you adopt a policy of *assuming constructive intent*. You might be assuming that the speaker is not trying to do their best thinking, or seeking a genuine solution. In fact, they are likely to be trying to think as well as they can. Assume that they are trying to be positive, and give appropriate feedback. One result, among others, is that the speaker will be encouraged to be more constructive.

The more formal the conversation, the more likely that your feedback will be a single, lengthy contribution. You need to choose carefully when to give your feedback. Too early, and you may close the conversation down prematurely. Too late, and the effect may be lost. If in doubt, you can ask whether it's appropriate to start your feedback or whether the speaker wants to continue. Ask:

- **for permission to feed back;**
- **how the speaker sees the situation in summary;**
- **what the speaker sees as the key issue or problem.**

Only then should you launch into your own feedback.

Give your positive feedback before any negative feedback. Make your own objective clear and explain how your feedback relates to that objective. Feedback will naturally become more positive if you make it forward-looking: what you and the other person are trying to achieve, what you both want to do. The best negative feedback is about whatever is hindering progress towards the objective. You can productively ignore any other ideas that you happen to disagree with.

Feed back on ideas and information, rather than on the person. Support any comments you make with evidence. Focus on the key idea or aspect that you think would change the situation most strongly for the better. If you praise them, the speaker is more likely to accept the need to change their views or their behaviour.

5

The skills of persuasion

The ability to persuade and influence has never been in more demand among managers. The days of simply telling people what to do and expecting them to do it are long gone. Now you have to be able to 'sell your ideas'.

The key to effective persuasion is having powerful ideas and delivering them well. Ideas are the currency of communication. Information alone will never influence anyone to act. Only ideas have the power to persuade.

The old word for this power is rhetoric. Since ancient times, the art of rhetoric has taught people how to assemble and deliver their ideas. Few people – at least in Europe – now study rhetoric systematically. Yet, by applying a few simple principles, you can radically improve the quality of your persuasion.

Character, logic and passion

Aristotle, the grandfather of rhetoric, claimed that we can persuade in two ways: through the evidence that we can bring to support our case, and through what he called 'artistic' persuasion.

Evidence is whatever we can display to support our case. We might use documents or witnesses; these days, we might use the results of research or focus groups.

'Artistic' persuasion consists of three appeals using the skills of the persuader themselves:

- **appealing to their reason;**
- **appealing to the audience's sense of your character or reputation; and**
- **appealing to their emotions.**

Aristotle's names for these appeals – *ethos*, *logos* and *pathos* – have become well known.

Logic (*logos*)

Logic is the work of rational thought. By using *logos*, we are appealing to our audience's ability to reason. We construct an argument, creating reasons to support the case we are making and demonstrating that those reasons logically support the case. Logic comes in two forms: deductive and inductive. (More about logic later in this chapter.)

Character (*ethos*)

Rhetoricians realised very early on that people were swayed as much by passions and prejudices as by reason. For example, we tend to believe people whom we trust or respect. *Ethos* is the appeal to our audience through personality, reputation or personal credibility. Why should your listener believe what you are telling them? What are your qualifications for saying all this? Where is your experience and expertise? How does your reputation stand with them? What value can you add to the argument from your own experience? Your character creates the trust upon which you can build your argument.

Passion (*pathos*)

In the end, human beings are probably influenced to act more by their emotions than by anything else. Appealing to their feelings – *pathos* – is thus a vital element in any attempt to persuade.

We tend to think of appealing to emotion as manipulative. Part of our suspicion arises from the fact that this appeal must always be indirect or underhand. We can lay out our argument or our credentials openly, but we cannot *announce* to our audience that we are about to appeal to their emotions; they will immediately be put on their guard. Neither can we inspire an emotion by talking about it; we must present something external that will arouse emotion. A charitable appeal, for example, might seek to arouse people to donate by showing pictures of children dying in hospital, or animals in distress. Feeling the emotion – or displaying it – may be helpful, but a dispassionate presentation or description will often be more emotionally arousing than an emotional one.

Pathos thus has the reputation of being dishonest or unethical. And we know that speakers can inspire audiences to wildly irrational and dangerous behaviour by playing on their emotions. But the abuse of *pathos* doesn't mean we should avoid it. Persuading without emotion is unlikely to be effective, partly because it will seem inhuman (Mr Spock on *Star Trek* continually had this problem when trying to persuade his colleagues to act rationally).

The aim of *pathos* must be to arouse the emotional response that is appropriate to the case you are arguing. Emotion need not be overwhelming. If we allow the subject matter or the occasion to elicit emotion in the audience, we shall probably exercise *pathos* well.

All three of these qualities – character, reasoning and passion – must be present if you want to persuade someone. The *process* of working out how to persuade them consists of five key elements:

- identifying the core idea;
- arranging your ideas logically;
- developing an appropriate style in the language you use;
- remembering your ideas;
- delivering your ideas with words, visual cues and non-verbal behaviour.

What's the big idea?

If you want to persuade someone, you must have a message. What do you want to say? What's the big idea? You must know what idea you want to promote. A single governing idea is more likely to persuade your listener than a group of ideas, simply because one strong idea is easier to remember.

Begin by gathering ideas. Conduct imaginary conversations in your head and note down the kind of things you might say. Capture ideas as they occur to you and store them on a pad or in a file. Spend as much time as you can on this activity before the conversation itself.

Having captured and stored some ideas, ask three fundamental questions:

- *'What is my objective?'* **What do I want to achieve? What would I like to see happen?**
- *'Who am I talking to?'* **Why am I talking to this person about this objective? What do they already know? What more do they need to know? What do I want them to do? What kind of ideas will be most likely to convince them?**
- *'What is the most important thing I have to say to them?'* **If I were only allowed a few minutes with them, what would I say to convince them – or, at least, to persuade them to keep listening?**

Think hard about these three questions. Imagine that you had only a few *seconds* to get your message across. What would you say?

Try to create a single sentence. Remember that you can't express an idea without uttering a sentence. Above all, this idea should be *new* to the listener. After all, there's no point in trying to persuade them of something they already know or agree with!

Once you have decided on your message, consider whether you think it is appropriate both to your objective and to your listener. Does this sentence express what you want to say? Is it in language that the listener will understand easily? Is it simple enough?

Now test your message sentence. If you were to speak this sentence to your listener, would they ask you a question? If so, what would that question be? If your message is a clear one, it will provoke *one* of these three questions:

- 'Why?'
- 'How?'
- 'Which ones?'

If you can't imagine your listener asking any of these questions, they're unlikely to be interested in your message. So try another. If you can imagine them asking more than one of these questions, try to simplify your message.

Now work out how to bring your listener to the place where they will accept this message. You must 'bring them around to your way of thinking'. This means starting where the listener is standing and gently guiding them to where you want them to be. Once you are standing in the same place, there is a much stronger chance that you will see things the same way. Persuading them will become a great deal easier.

People will only be persuaded by ideas that interest them. Your listener will only be interested in your message because it answers some need or question that already exists in their mind. An essential element in delivering your message, then, is demonstrating that it relates to that need or that question.

Here is a simple four-point structure that will bring your listener to the point where they can accept your message. I remember it by using the letters SPQR.

Situation

Briefly tell the listener something they already know. Make a statement about the matter that you *know* they will agree with. This demonstrates that you are on their territory: you understand their situation and can appreciate their point of view. Try to state the Situation in such a way that the listener expects to hear more. Think of this as a kind of 'Once upon a time...'. It's an opener, a scene-setting statement that prepares them for what's to come.

Problem

Now identify a Problem that has arisen within the Situation. The listener may know about the Problem; they may not. But they certainly should know about it! In other words, the Problem should be their problem at least as much as yours.

What's the problem?

Situation	Problem
Stable, agreed	Something's gone wrong
status quo	Something could go wrong
	Something's changed
	Something could change
	Something new has arisen
	Someone has a different point of view
	We don't know what to do
	There are a number of things we could do

Problems, of course, come in many shapes and sizes. It's important that you identify a Problem that the listener will recognise. It must clearly relate to the Situation that you have set up: it poses a threat to it or creates a challenge within it.

Problems can be positive as well as negative. You may want to alert your listener to an opportunity that has arisen within the Situation.

Question

The Problem causes the listener to ask a Question (or would do so, if they were aware of it). Once again, the listener may or may not be asking the Question. If they are, you are better placed to be able to answer it. If they are not, you may have to carefully get them to agree that this Question is worth asking.

What's the question?

Situation	Problem	Question
Stable, agreed status quo	Something's gone wrong	What do we do?
	Something could go wrong	How do we stop it?
	Something's changed	How do we adjust to it?
	Something could change	How do we prepare for it?
	Something new has arisen	What can we do?
	Someone has a different point of view	Who's right?
	We don't know what to do	What do we do? or How do we choose?
	There are a number of things we we could do	Which course do we take?

Response

Your Response or answer to the Question is your message. In other words, the message should naturally emerge as the logical and powerful answer to the Question raised in the listener's mind by the Problem!

SPQR is a classic story-telling framework. It is also well known as a method management consultants use in the introductions to their proposals. The trick is to take your listener through the four stages *quickly*. Don't be tempted to fill out the story with lots of detail. As you use SPQR, remember these three key points:

1. SPQR should remind the listener rather than persuade them. Until you get to the message, you shouldn't include any idea that you would need to prove.
2. Think of SPQR as a story. Keep it moving. Keep the listener's interest.
3. Adapt the stages of the story to the needs of the listener. Make sure that they agree to the first three stages without difficulty. Make sure that you are addressing their needs, values, priorities. Put everything in their terms.

Arranging your ideas

Logic is the method by which you assemble ideas into a coherent structure. So you must have a number of key ideas that support the message you have chosen. Ideally, they are answers to the question you can imagine your listener asking when you utter your message.

Finding your key ideas

If your message provokes the listener to ask:	Your key ideas will be:
'Why?'	Reasons, benefits or causes
'How?'	Methods, ways to do something, procedures
'Which ones?'	These ones: items in a list

There are two ways to organise ideas logically. They can be organised deductively, in a sequence, and inductively, in a pyramid.

Arguing deductively

Deductive logic takes the form of a syllogism: an argument in which a conclusion is inferred from two statements (see Figure 5.1). To argue deductively:

- **make a statement;**
- **make a second statement that relates to the first – by commenting on either the subject of the first statement, or on what you have said about that subject;**
- **state the implication of these two statements being true simultaneously. This conclusion is your message.**

Arguing inductively

Inductive logic works by stating a governing idea and then delivering a group of other ideas that the governing idea summarises. Another name for this kind of logic is *grouping and summarising*.

Figure 5.1   Some examples of deductive reasoning

Inductive logic creates pyramids of ideas (see Figure 5.2). You can test the logic of the structure by asking whether the ideas in any one group are answers to the question that the summarising idea provokes. (You've done this already when formulating your message.) That question will be one of three: 'Why?', 'How?' or 'Which ones?'

Inductive logic tends to be more powerful in business than deductive logic. Deductive logic brings two major risks with it.

1. It demands real patience on the part of the listener. If you put too many ideas into your sequence, you may stretch their patience to breaking point.
2. You may undermine your own argument. Each stage in the deductive sequence is an invitation to the listener to disagree. And they only have to disagree with one of the stages for the whole sequence to collapse.

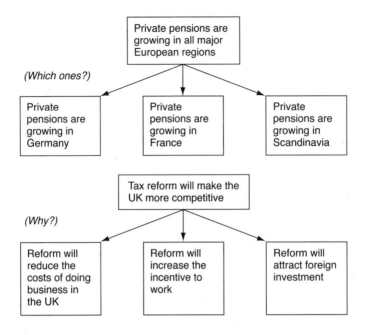

(Which ones?)

(Why?)

Figure 5.2   Some examples of inductive reasoning

Inductive logic avoids both of these perils. First, it doesn't strain the listener's patience so much because the main idea – the message – appears at the beginning. Secondly, a pyramid is less likely to collapse than a strung-out sequence of ideas. It's easier to construct than a deductive sequence because you can see more clearly whether your other ideas support your message. And the message has a good chance of surviving even if one of the supporting ideas is removed. Pyramids of ideas satisfy our thirst for answers now and evidence later. They allow you to be more creative in assembling your ideas and they put the message right at the front.

Deductive logic is only really useful for establishing whether something is true. Inductive logic can also help you to establish whether something is *worth doing*.

Expressing your ideas

It's not enough to have coherent ideas, logically organised. You have to bring the ideas alive in the listener's mind. You have to use words to create pictures and feelings that will stimulate their senses as well as their brain.

We don't remember words. We forget nearly everything others say. But we *do* remember images – particularly images that excite sensory impressions and feelings. If you can excite your listener's imagination through the senses and stimulate some feeling in them, you will be able to plant the accompanying idea in their long-term memory.

Memory = image + feeling

The word 'image', of course, powerfully suggests something visual. But you can create *impressions* through any of the five senses: sight, hearing, touch, smell and taste. Some people will be convinced by pictures; others will only be persuaded if they hear the words come out of their own mouth. Others again will only remember and learn by touching: they are the 'hands-on' people who demand demonstrations and practice.

Neuro-linguistic programming (NLP) works on the basis of people's natural sensory preferences for receiving information. NLP seeks to develop this awareness of sensory preference into a systematic approach to communicating.

Even without training or study, however, you can become more attuned to the way you respond to ideas with your senses. Whenever you are seeking to persuade someone with an idea, think about how each of the five senses might respond to it. Try to create an impression of the idea that will appeal to one or other of the senses. You'll find that the idea comes magically alive.

Examples

Perhaps the simplest way to bring an idea alive is to offer a concrete example. Find an instance where the idea has been put into practice, or where it has created real results – either useful or disastrous.

Examples can be powerfully and immediately persuasive. Concrete instances and applications of ideas make us take the ideas more seriously. It may be easier to befuddle your listener by talking in abstract terms; but a single clear example will clarify your idea immediately.

Stories

Stories are special kinds of examples. They lend weight to the example by making it personal. They also have the benefit of entertaining the listener, keeping them in suspense and releasing an emotional response with a surprising revelation. Much everyday persuasion and explanation is in the form of stories: gossip, jokes, speculation, 'war stories' or plain rumour.

Stories work best when they are concrete and personal. Tell your own, authentic stories. They will display your character and your passion. They will also be easier to remember! If you want to tell another person's story, explain that it's not yours and tell it swiftly. A story will persuade your listener if it has a clear point. Without a point, it can become counterproductive: an annoying diversion and a waste of time. You may need to make it clear: 'and the point of the story is...'.

Using metaphors

Using metaphors, as discussed in Chapter 3, is the technique of expressing one thing in terms of another. Metaphors allow you to see things in new ways by showing how they relate to others. The most persuasive metaphors are those that make a direct appeal to the senses and to experience.

Metaphors create meaning. They burn ideas into your listener's mind (that's a metaphor!). They help listeners to remember by creating pictures (or sounds, or tastes, or smells) that they can store in their mind (I'm using the metaphor of a cupboard or library to explain some part of the mind's working).

Remembering your ideas

Memory played a vital role in the art of rhetoric in the days before printing. With no ready means of making notes or easy access to books, remembering ideas and their relationships was an essential skill. Whole systems of memory were invented to help people store information and recall it at will.

These days, memory hardly seems to figure as a life skill – except for passing examinations. It seems that technology has taken its place. There is no *need* to remember: merely to read and store e-mails, pick up messages (voice and text) on the mobile, plug in, surf and download...

However, memory still plays an important part in persuading others. If you can't begin to persuade someone without a heap of spreadsheets and a briefcase full of project designs to refer to, don't start. Nobody was ever persuaded by watching someone recite from a sheaf of notes.

Find a way to bring the ideas off paper and into your head. Give yourself some clear mental signposts so that you can find your way from one idea to the next. Write a few notes on a card or on the back of your hand. Draw a mindmap. Make it colourful. If you've assembled a mental pyramid, draw it on a piece of paper and carry it with you. Have some means available to draw your thoughts as you explain them: a notepad, a flip chart, a whiteboard. Invite the other person to join in: encourage them to think of this as the shape of their thinking.

Delivering effectively

Delivery means supporting your ideas with effective behaviour. Chapter 2 showed how non-verbal communication is a vital component in creating understanding. When you are seeking to persuade, your behaviour will be the most persuasive thing about you. If you are saying one thing but your body is saying another, no one will believe your words.

Think about the style of delivery your listener might prefer. Do they favour a relaxed, informal conversational style or a more formal, presentational delivery? Are they interested in the broad picture or do they want lots of supporting detail? Will they want to ask questions?

Delivery is broadly about three kinds of activity. Think about the way you use your:

- **eyes;**
- **voice;**
- **body.**

Effective eye contact

People speak more with their eyes than with their voice. Maintain eye contact with your listener. If you are talking to more than one person, include everybody with your eyes. Focus on their eyes: don't look through them. There are two occasions when you might break eye contact: when you are thinking about what to say next; and when you are looking at notes, a mindmap or some other object of common attention.

Using your voice

Your voice will sound more persuasive if it is not too high, too fast or too thin. Work to regulate and strengthen your breathing while you speak. Breathe deep and slow. Let your voice emerge more from your body than from your throat. Slow down the pace of your voice, too: it can be all too easy to gabble when you are involved in an argument or nervous about the other person's reactions. The more body your voice has, and the more measured your vocal delivery, the more convincing you will sound.

Persuasive body language

Your face, your limbs and your body posture will all contribute to the total effect your ideas have on the listener. To start with, try not to frown. Keep your facial muscles moving and pay attention to keeping your neck muscles relaxed. Use your hands to paint pictures, to help you find the right words and express yourself fully.

Professional persuaders observe their listeners' behaviour and quietly mirror it. If you are relaxed with the other person, such mirroring will tend to happen naturally: you may find you are crossing your legs in similar ways or moving your arms in roughly the same way. Try consciously to adapt your own posture and movement to that of the person listening to you. Do more: take the lead. Don't sit back or close your body off when you are seeking to persuade; bring yourself forward, open yourself up and present yourself along with your ideas.

6

Interviews: holding a formal conversation

Every manager holds interviews. To be able to hold a structured interview with someone to achieve a clear goal is a fundamental managerial skill.

When is an interview not an interview?

The word 'interview' simply means 'looking between us': an interview is an exchange of views. Any conversation – conducted well – is such an exchange. Interviews differ from other conversations in that they:

- **are held for a very specific reason;**
- **aim at a particular outcome;**
- **are more carefully and consciously structured;**
- **must usually cover predetermined matters of concern;**
- **are called and led by one person – the interviewer;**
- **are usually recorded.**

This chapter will look at the following four types of interview:

- **appraisal;**
- **delegation;**
- **coaching;**
- **counselling.**

Each type of interview will demand a range of skills from you, the interviewer. All of the skills of enquiry and persuasion that have been explored so far in this book will come into play at some point.

Preparing for the interview

Prepare for the interview by considering three questions:

- **What's my objective?**
- **What do I need?**
- **When and where?**

What's my objective?

What do you want to achieve in the interview? You must decide, for you are calling the interview. Do you want to discipline a member of staff for risking an accident, or influence their attitude to safety? Are you trying to offload a boring routine task or seeking to delegate as a way of developing a member of your team? Are you counselling or coaching?

Setting a clear objective is the only way you will be able to measure the interview's success. And it is essential if you want to be able to decide on the style and structure of the interview.

What do I need?

Think about the information you will need before and during the interview. Think also about what information the interviewee will need. What are the key areas you need to cover? In what order? What questions do you need to ask?

You may also need other kinds of equipment to help you: notepads, flip charts, files, samples of material or machinery. You may even need a witness to ensure that the interview is seen to be conducted professionally and fairly.

When and where?

When do you propose to interview? For how long? The time of day is as important as the day you choose. Certain times of day are notoriously difficult for interview: after lunch, for example – or during lunch! Remember also that an interview that goes on too long will become counterproductive.

The quality of the interview will be strongly influenced by its venue. You may decide that your office is too formal or intimidating; on the other hand, interviewing in a crowded public area or in the pub can destroy the sense of privacy that any interview should encourage. You may decide to conduct some parts of an interview in different places.

Think also about the climate you set up for the interviewee. Sitting them on a low chair, beyond a desk, facing a sunny window, with nowhere to put a cup of coffee, will obviously set up an unpleasant atmosphere.

Structuring the interview

Interviews, like other conversations, naturally fall into a structure. Interviewers sometimes try to press an interview forward towards a result without allowing enough time for the early stages.

Every interview can be structured using the WASP structure that was examined in Chapter 3. This structure reinforces the fact that both stages of thinking are important.

- *Welcome (first-stage thinking).* At the start of the interview, state your objective, set the scene and establish your relationship. 'Why are we talking about this matter? Why us?' Do whatever you can to help the interviewee relax. Make sure the interviewee understands the rules you are establishing, and agrees to them.
- *Acquire (first-stage thinking).* The second step is information gathering. Concentrate on finding out as much as possible about the matter, as the interviewee sees it. Your task is to listen. Ask questions only to keep the interview on course or to encourage the interviewee further down a useful road. Take care not to judge or imply that you are making any decision.
- *Supply (second-stage thinking).* Now, at the third step, the interview has moved on from information gathering to joint problem solving. Review options for action. It's important at this stage of the interview to remind yourselves of the objective that you set at the start.
- *Part (second-stage thinking).* Finally, make a decision. You and the interviewee work out what you have agreed. State explicitly the interview's outcome: the action that will result from it. The essence of the parting stage is that you explicitly agree what is going to happen next. What is going to happen? Who will do it? Is there a deadline? Who is going to check on progress?

What about after the interview? In many cases, you may need time to put your thoughts in order and make decisions. Indeed, it might be entirely inappropriate to decide – or to tell the interviewee what you have decided – at the end of the interview itself. The interviewee, too, may need time to reflect on the interview. Nevertheless, you must tell the interviewee what you expect the next step to be and make sure that they agree to it.

After the interview

- **Make your notes immediately.** There's no general rule about whether to take notes during the interview, except that note-taking should not interfere with listening to the interviewee unduly.
- **Carry out any actions you have agreed** and follow up on actions agreed by the interviewee.
- **Review your own performance as an interviewer.** What went well? What could have been better? Above all, did you achieve the objective you set yourself? A few moments reviewing your own performance can certainly help you in later interviews.

Types of interview

These are a selection of the most common interviews you will hold as a manager. Every interview is analysed in terms of the four-stage WASP structure. Whatever kind of interview you are holding, use all the skills of enquiry that we have explored in Chapter 4:

- paying attention;
- treating the interviewee as an equal;
- cultivating ease;
- encouraging;
- asking quality questions;
- rationing information;
- giving positive feedback.

Appraisal

An appraisal interview is one of the most important you hold as a manager. It's vital that both you and the jobholder prepare thoroughly for the interview.

Preparing for the interview

You should study the jobholder's job description and the standards of performance that you have set up. If targets have been set and regularly reviewed, think about these with care. The key questions to ask at this stage are:

- **What results has the jobholder achieved?**
- **Where has the jobholder exceeded expectations or shown real progress?**
- **Which results have not been achieved? Can you suggest why?**

Make sure that you tell the jobholder what you are doing to prepare and invite them to prepare in a similar way. Ask them, well in advance, to consider their own performance over the appraised period, and to note successes, failures and anything in between!

The essence of a successful appraisal is the comparison of the two sets of ideas: yours and the jobholder's. You are aiming for shared understanding: an agreement about the jobholder's performance and potential for the future.

Holding the interview

Don't kill the appraisal off at an early stage by descending into adversarial conversation. Be ready with the Ladder of Inference (see Chapter 3) to take any potential controversy into a more careful examination of facts and feelings.

Welcome

Review standards, targets, the job description and any other aspects of performance that you have both looked at. Relate them: take comparisons and talk about what's been achieved, and what has not happened. Stick to the known facts and make sure that you agree them.

Your questions to the jobholder might include:

- **How do you feel your job has been going since we last spoke?**
- **What do you feel you do best?**
- **Where do you have real problems?**
- **How relevant is the job description?**

Acquire

Open up the interview by asking the jobholder for their views and withholding your own. Review the possible reasons for achievement or lack of it. Open up the interview to include matters of competency, skills, training and external circumstances.

Questions at this stage might include:

- **What are your strong points?**
- **Where do you think you could develop?**
- **What particular problems have you had? How do you think you could have handled them differently?**

Look for possibilities rather than uttering closed judgements. Instead of saying, for example, 'You're aggressive with our customers', you might say 'Some of our customers seem to perceive your behaviour as aggressive. What do you think about that?' Use behaviour as the basis for your comments. Have evidence to hand. Be ready to reinterpret the evidence from the jobholder's point of view.

Supply

This is the problem-solving part of the interview. Analyse what you have found, and focus on opportunities for action, change and improvement. Generate alternatives. Seek agreement on what could be done. You might be looking for new moves towards targets, performance standards or even amendments to the job description.

Questions at this stage include:

- **What might we do to alter our targets or standards?**
- **Do we need to rewrite any part of the job description?**
- **How could the job be improved? Have you any ideas?**

Part

You and the jobholder confirm your agreement and part on the clear understanding that these actions are recorded and will be monitored.

Look back at the essential elements of a conversation for action in Chapter 3. Remember that you will gain more commitment from the jobholder if you make requests and invite them to give a considered response.

Don't complete any forms during the interview. It will take too long and distract you from your real business. Take time to fill out any paperwork carefully, after the interview has ended. You need time to assemble your thoughts and summarise them in your mind. You should, of course, at least show any completed paperwork to the jobholder and involve them in any changes.

You must make sure that you carry out any actions that you agree to in the interview: support, procedural changes, delegation or training. If you do not, you undermine both your own authority and the credibility of the appraisal process itself. And you will find it harder next time to generate the respect and trust that form the basis of the whole system.

Handling poor performance

You will sometimes have to handle poor performance. Anyone can perform under par at times. Usually some underachieving can be tolerated, but persistent or serious shortfalls need action. Avoiding the issue will not make it go away.

What you may see as poor performance is not necessarily the jobholder's fault. In fact, it's unrewarding to think in terms of blame or fault if you detect poor performance. Of course, it may be a genuine case of misconduct; but the circumstances of poor performance are likely to be more complex. An effective manager will look deeper and not jump to conclusions.

First, establish the gap. What is the standard that isn't being met? Is the gap sufficient enough, and consistent enough, to warrant action?

Now establish possible reasons for the gap in achievement. There are three main reasons why jobholders can under-perform:

- *Domestic circumstances.* **They may be in poor health or suffering some emotional instability, owing to family or personal problems.**
- *Poor management.* **The job has not been sufficiently explained. Planning has been poor. The job may have changed in ways that don't make sense to the jobholder. Resources may be lacking. Discipline may be slack. Physical conditions may make working to standard very difficult. You may be managing the job poorly – as may another manager.**
- *Lack of organisational 'fit'.* **The jobholder may be unhappy in the team, or the team unhappy with the jobholder. So-called 'personality clashes' may be getting in the way, or a sense of natural justice may be being abused.**

Having established the gap and the reason for it, you must set out with the jobholder to work out a plan for closing the gap. Where are the opportunities for improvement? How might you be able to help? Think of this part of the interview as joint problem solving. Find a course of action that the jobholder can agree to. Only they can behave differently, so they must decide what to do.

They may be able to make substantial improvements in stages. Explain that you will be available to help.

Record your agreement and don't forget to follow up on agreed action.

Delegation

Delegation is deliberately choosing to give somebody authority to do something you could do yourself. It is not just 'handing out work'. You give somebody a responsibility: the task to be performed; and you devolve authority: the power to make other decisions and to take action to carry out the responsibility. Successful delegation involves matching responsibility with authority. Anybody who manages will know how difficult this can be – as will any parent or carer.

Preparing for the interview: working out what to delegate

Review your own objectives. Now distinguish between the activities you can delegate and those for which you must take personal responsibility. Obvious candidates for delegation include:

- **routine tasks;**
- **time-consuming tasks – research, testing, administrative or coordinating activities;**
- **complete tasks that can be delegated as a block of work;**
- **communication tasks – letters, promotional material, telephone calls.**

Delegate tasks that might be tedious for you but prove a real challenge to somebody else. Do not delegate:

- **tasks completely beyond the skills and experience of the person concerned;**

- strategic, policy, confidential or security matters;
- tasks involving discipline over the person's peers.

Having decided what to delegate, ask these questions:

- **What skills, experience, expertise and qualifications are necessary for the task?**
- **Whose skills profile best matches the need?**
- **What further training or support would be necessary?**

Look for people's interest in work that they haven't already done, or have maybe shown some aptitude for in unusual circumstances (covering for somebody else, coping in a crisis). Look for abilities that are exercised elsewhere: in another part of their work, or perhaps outside work.

Holding the interview

As with other kinds of interview, you can structure the interview to give yourself the best possible chance of success.

- *Welcome*. **Explain the purpose of the interview. Begin by making the request. 'I should like to discuss with you the possibility of delegating x.' Explain the task you are considering delegating, and why you have thought of the interviewee as the best person to do the task. Explain that their position is an open one: they should feel under no obligation until they have clearly understood the question you are asking.**
- *Acquire*. **Ask the jobholder to explore their understanding of the issue and how they might see themselves relating to it. Does it fit with other responsibilities that they currently carry? Can they see it as an opportunity to grow and develop new skills? Examine, too, the standards of performance. Are they appropriate or attainable? Would training be necessary?**
- *Supply*. **Explore with the jobholder the opportunities for taking on this new task. This is joint problem solving**

again, looking at the new arrangement in terms of how it might work, how you might help and how the interviewee might make the work more their own.
- *Part.* Now make your request a formal one. Give timescales or deadlines, as well as conditions of satisfaction: standards or targets to be achieved, how you will monitor progress and check for success.

Make it clear to the delegate that they have four possible responses.

- They can accept the request and make a commitment. 'I promise that I will do *x* by time *y*.'
- They can decline. They must be free to say 'No', while at the same time being clear of the consequences of a refusal.
- They can decide to commit later. 'I'll get back to you by time *z*, when I will give you a definite response.'
- They can make a counter-offer. 'I'm not willing to do *x*; however, I can promise you that I will do *w* (or maybe part of *x*) by time *y*.'

The result of this interview should be a clear commitment by the delegate to action: to the task originally intended for delegation, to part of the task, to another task, or to refusal.

In accepting a newly delegated responsibility, the delegate must be clear about three limits on their action:

- *Objectives.* The broad objectives of the task, the specific targets, conditions of satisfaction and timescales should all be made explicit.
- *Policy.* 'Rules and regulations.' The manner in which the task is carried out must conform to any legal, contractual or policy guidelines under which the organisation operates.
- *Limits of authority.* This is critically important. The delegate must know clearly where their authority

extends and where it ends: what powers they have for hiring or using staff, their budgetary authority, the resources available to them, their access to information, their power to take decisions without referral.

Finally, you as the manager must give the delegate full confidence to do the task. Make it plain that you will:

- give any support that you or they consider necessary;
- provide any training that may be needed;
- be available for consultation or advice;
- make the delegation public knowledge.

Coaching

Coaching is improving performance. The aim of a coaching interview is to help the coachee think for themselves, fostering greater awareness and hence greater responsibility. Fostering awareness is the first stage of coaching and involves looking at:

- what is going on;
- the goals;
- dynamics and relationships between the coachee and others;
- wider organisational issues;
- the coachee's own feelings; fears, emotions, desires, intuitions, capabilities.

Fostering responsibility is the second stage of coaching and involves second-stage thinking: thinking about what to do. So at this stage, coaching encourages the coachee to think about:

- ideas for action;
- opportunities for change or growth;
- deciding what to do and how to do it;
- taking action.

The coach's role is to ask questions. Instructing will tend to generate a minimal response: the action carried out, but little more. Asking a question focuses attention, increases awareness and encourages the coachee to take responsibility. Asking questions also helps the coach. Instead of forging ahead with a sequence of orders, the coach can use questions to follow the coachee's train of thought, their interest or enthusiasm, their emotional reactions – and adapt the coaching accordingly.

The most effective questions are those that encourage the coachee to think for themselves. Questions that point up the coachee's ignorance or subservience are unhelpful. The best coaching questions are open, non-judgemental and *specific*. Use the 'W' questions: 'What? Where? When? Who? How many? How much?' Avoid 'Why?' and 'How?' They will tend to imply judgement, analysis or criticism: all of them forms of second-stage thinking. If necessary, 'Why?' can become 'What were the reasons for' and 'How?' might be better put as 'What were the steps that...?'

During second-stage thinking, the same kinds of questions can serve to focus on what the coachee will do next, how, when, where and so on.

The Ladder of Inference is a useful tool in this process. Walking the coachee down the ladder from beliefs or assumptions to specific observations will encourage a wider awareness; walking up the ladder through meanings, judgement and belief to action will strengthen motivation and a sense of responsibility for future actions.

Holding the interview

There are four parts to the coaching process. The WASP interview structure now takes on a new name, based around the word GROW:

- *Goal* setting: for the session and for the coachee's development;
- *Reality* analysis: to explore the current situation for difficulties and opportunities;

- *Options* for future courses of action;
- *What* to do: a 'hard' decision on action, *when* and by *whom.*

Goal setting

The initial task is to decide the purpose of the coaching: to establish your goal, both for the coaching session itself and for the performance issue being coached.

Think of the coachee's goals as statements beginning 'How to...'. Generate as many new 'How to' statements as you can from the original goal. This helps you to explore the coachee's deeper values, their higher aspirations and longer-term ambitions.

Now categorise these numerous 'How to' statements. Some will be 'end goals'; others will be 'performance goals', measurable levels of performance that may set you on the path to an end goal or prove that you've achieved it. All of them are revealing: but you will only be able to choose one or two for immediate coaching. The best goals to choose, for practical purposes, are those that generate the greatest creative tension between goal and reality. Like the tension in a taut elastic band that stores potential energy, it is creative tension that will provide the energy for movement. Which goals excite the coachee most? Which generate the most commitment?

Reality checking

Creative tension depends as much on a clear perception of reality as on a clear goal. Look reality coolly in the face. Be objective; avoid judgement. Instead of describing past performance, for example, as 'bad' or 'inadequate', focus on the specific aspects of it that need improvement. Walk the coachee down the Ladder of Inference and offer verifiable, measurable observations:

- **'What have you tried so far?'**
- **'What were the results?'**
- **'Exactly how much under target did you come in?'**

- 'What resources do you lack?'
- 'When did you last check the situation?'
- 'Where were the actual difficulties?'

Remember that a good deal of current reality is inner reality. Follow where the coachee's concerns take you and (gently) investigate their emotional responses.

- 'How did you feel when you tried...?'
- 'What emotions arise when you talk about...?'
- 'Is there anything you're afraid of?'
- 'How do you think you might be preventing yourself from achieving more?'

Options for action

This is potentially the most creative part of the coaching process. Your purpose here is to find as many options for action as possible, in order to choose specific, realistic 'next steps'.

'The opponent within one's own head' can be a powerful censor:

- 'It can't be done.'
- 'We can't do it like that.'
- 'They would never agree to it.'
- 'It will be too expensive.'
- 'Altogether too risky/disruptive/complicated/radical.'
- 'I don't have the time.'
- 'That's already been tried – and look what happened.'

You might counter these objections with 'What if' questions:

- 'What if we could do it?'
- 'What if this barrier didn't exist?'
- 'What if we could get them to agree?'
- 'What if we found a budget?'
- 'What if we managed the risk/minimised disruption/ made it simpler...?'

- 'What if we reallocated resources?'
- 'What if we tried again?'

Keep your options open:

'What else could you do?'
'Could you do it differently?'
'Are there other ways of meeting this target or goal?'

Carefully examine the costs and benefits of the action; list its positive, negative and interesting aspects. Don't limit yourselves to one option: perhaps you can merge two or more as a realistic course of action, or schedule options as immediate and longer term.

What to do

This part of the coaching process is about drawing up a detailed action plan:

- 'What are you going to do?'
- 'When will you do it?'
- 'Will this action (or series of actions) move you towards your goal?'
- 'What barriers might you have to overcome?'
- 'Who else will be involved?'
- 'What support do you need? Where will you find it?'
- 'What other consequences are there of this course of action, and how do we deal with them?'

And it is vital for the coach to ask a final question:

- 'What can I do to help?'

It is a good idea to document the agreed action plan, and even sign it, to confirm that the coachee is committed to carrying it through. Build in a review date to monitor progress.

Counselling

Counselling, like coaching, helps someone to help themselves. Unlike coaching, you are not helping to develop a skill, but rather helping to resolve a situation that the person sees as a problem.

Counselling is not giving advice. As a counsellor, your role is to provide a different perspective from which to try out ideas. The counselled person (I suppose we must call them the 'counsellee'!) must find their own solution and exercise their own responsibility. Neither the counsellor nor the counsellee knows the answer at the start of the counselling interview. The answer emerges from the interview itself.

Counselling always relies on the assumption that the counsellee has the skills, knowledge and – deep down – the desire to find a solution. It also assumes that these skills and qualities are impeded in some way. The impediment may be no more than the belief that the counsellee doesn't know what to do.

The skills of counselling

The skills of counselling are not unlike the skills you use every day when people tell you about their problems. The difference is that you must behave professionally; in other words, honestly, consistently, and without prejudice. Your contribution should be well informed and appropriate to the situation.

Counselling, more than any other managerial interview, demands deep listening skills. Indeed, you may be required to do nothing but listen. Beyond the essential skill of listening, there are two main skills that come to the fore in counselling:

- **reflecting;**
- **confronting.**

Used well, they will all help to make the interview more productive.

Reflecting

Counsellors use reflection in three main ways. They reflect:

- **what people seem to be feeling;**
- **their words, the content of what they have said;**
- **the implied content.**

These are such vital tools of counselling that it is worth looking at each of them separately.

Reflecting feelings   This is probably the most useful, and the technique likely to be used first in a counselling session. It always clarifies the issue being discussed and it helps the speaker to know that the listener really does understand. Frequently it needs to be no more than a few words:

- **'You feel angry.'**
- **'You seem to be distracted.'**
- **'Perhaps you are confused.'**

Reflecting the speaker's words   This is a very simple and effective technique, enabling you to prompt the counsellee without running the risk of the discussion 'going off track'. Early in a session, it can 'open up issues'; at other times it can help to break through a 'block'. The counsellor listens carefully for emotionally charged words, those given undue emphasis, or for which the speaker's voice fades or becomes barely audible. Simply repeating those words can have magical effects.

Reflecting content   The trick here is simply to repeat what the counsellee has just told you: 'You say that you are not being challenged enough.' It usually results in an elaboration of the point that has been made and provides a way forward. Perhaps the counsellee can't quite bring themselves to say it, but they will talk volubly on the subject if you legitimise it for them.

Confronting

Use this technique with great care. It may consist simply of asking for concrete detail to support an allegation or an expression of vague feeling. It may involve pointing out apparent contradictions: between what the counsellee is saying and what they said earlier; between what they are saying and the way they are saying it; between words and body language. Remember that you are confronting perceptions in order to root out possible new ones. You are not confronting to criticise or to degrade the counsellee in any way.

Holding the interview

The four stages of counselling are very like those of coaching. The main difference between them is a matter of emphasis. Coaching is about reaching a goal and improving in some way; counselling is essentially about removing some obstacle or difficulty and simply being able to move on.

Welcome

You need to establish at the outset a positive relationship between counsellor and counsellee. The counsellee will almost certainly be feeling vulnerable and anything you can do to put them at their ease – to create the trust and respect that they need – is essential. Ask 'What is the problem?' (as the counsellee sees it), 'Where is the "blockage"?'

Acquire

Some aspect of this problem is probably 'buried': either because the counsellee is unwilling to bring it to the surface (for fear of the consequences) or because they are not aware of it. Help them to step back and examine the possibilities of the situation by asking questions such as:

- **'Why do you think you feel this way?'**
- **'What kind of response do you think you might get if you told X about this?'**

- 'Who else has contributed to the problem?'
- 'How do you think this has arisen?'
- 'What might be the cause of the problem?'

You might consider making the interview more creative at this stage by asking the counsellee to think about the problem in radically different ways:

- 'What does this problem look like?'
- 'If you were the problem, how would you feel?'
- 'Can you think of another way of expressing the problem?'

In some situations, you may be able to help the counsellee to transform the problem in some radical way. They probably see the problem as a burden that they must bear, or an obstacle that they must overcome. A key stage in taking ownership of the problem is to see it instead as a goal for which they can take responsibility.

Invite the counsellee to try to frame the problem as a 'How to' statement. The idea is that by doing so the problem becomes expressed as an objective: a way forward that the counsellee might want to take. A 'How to' statement also implies multiple possibilities of movement: if you are asking 'how to' achieve a goal, the mind immediately responds with 'well, you might... or you might...' and so on.

Turning an obstacle into a goal is at the very heart of the counselling process. You must use all your skill and sensitivity to manage this most crucial part of the process. A counsellee may all too easily feel pressure at this point to take ownership of a problem when they have no desire to do so.

Supply

Now you must supply some possible courses of action and consider their consequences. The counsellee should be moving from emotion to a more considered attitude without any pressure from you. They should be visualising various results and how they would feel about them. They should be feeling more enabled to choose a course of action.

Part

At this last stage of the counselling interview, you are not making a request – beyond the simple request that the counsellee makes a decision. Now that they can see their situation more clearly and have assessed various options, they need to make a move. It might be a very small one; it might be the beginnings of a planned strategy. (Many of my own more stressful problems seem to dissolve in the face of a clear plan.)

If you have helped someone to make a clear plan that they are motivated to act on, then your counselling has succeeded. You can also use this stage of the interview to help the counsellee reflect on the skills, knowledge, experience and personal qualities that are likely to help them through.

7

Making a presentation

Think of a presentation as a formal conversation. Speaking to groups is a notoriously stressful activity. Most people spend hours of their time holding conversations. Something strange seems to happen, however, when they're called upon to talk to a group of people formally. A host of irrational – and maybe not so irrational fears – raise their ugly heads.

What do you fear most?

A recent study in the United States asked people about their deepest fears. The results were interesting. Here they are, in order:

- speaking to groups;
- heights;
- insects and bugs;
- financial problems;

- deep water;
- sickness;
- death;
- flying;
- loneliness;
- dogs.

(From *The Book of Lists*, David Wallechinsky)

I think that one of the main causes of this anxiety is that you put yourself on the spot when you present. The audience will be judging, not just your ideas and your evidence, but you as well. People may not remember reports or spreadsheets easily, but a presentation can make a powerful impression that lasts. If the presenter seemed nervous, incompetent or ill-informed, that reputation will stick – at least until the next presentation.

You, the presenter, are at the heart of it. An effective presenter puts themself centre-stage. An ineffective presenter tries to hide behind notes, a lectern, slides or computer-generated graphics. To become more effective, you need to take control of the three core elements of the event:

- **the material;**
- **the audience;**
- **yourself.**

Whatever you are presenting, you will also need to use all the skills of persuasion that we explored in Chapter 5:

- **working out your big idea: your message;**
- **validating your message using SPQR (situation–problem–question–response, see Chapter 5);**
- **arranging your ideas coherently;**
- **expressing your ideas vividly;**
- **remembering your ideas;**
- **delivering well.**

Putting yourself on show

Think a bit more about this business of nerves. What's going on in those minutes and hours before you stand up and make your presentation? What is your body saying?

That nervous, jittery feeling is caused by adrenalin. This is a hormone secreted by your adrenal glands (near your kidneys). Adrenalin causes your arteries to constrict, which increases your blood pressure and stimulates the heart. Why stimulate the heart? To give you extra energy. When do you need extra energy? When you're in danger. Adrenalin release is an evolved response to threat.

Adrenalin has two other effects. It increases your concentration – particularly useful when making a presentation. Less usefully, adrenalin also stimulates excretion of body waste. This decreases your body weight, giving you a slight advantage when it comes to running! That's why you want to visit the toilet immediately before presenting.

Your anxiety is probably more about your relationship with the audience than about what you have to say. In the moments before you present, you may find yourself suffering from one or more of the following conditions:

- **demophobia – a fear of people;**
- **laliophobia – a fear of speaking;**
- **katagelophobia – a fear of ridicule.**

Check your condition against this list of adrenalin-related symptoms:

- **rapid pulse;**
- **shallow breathing;**
- **muscle spasms in the throat, knees and hands;**
- **dry mouth;**
- **cold extremities;**
- **dilated pupils;**

- sweaty palms;
- blurred vision;
- nausea.

And the worst of it is that, however much you suffer, the audience will forget virtually everything you say! That's the bad news. The good news is that you're not alone. Every presenter – indeed, every performer – suffers from nerves. Many actors and musicians talk about the horror of nerves and the fact that experience never seems to make them better.

The best news is that nerves are there to help you. They are telling you that this presentation matters – and that *you* matter. You are the medium through which the audience will understand your ideas. You *should* feel nervous. If you don't, you aren't taking the presentation seriously and you are in danger of letting your concentration slip.

Preparing for the presentation

The trick is not to try to dispel the nerves, but to use them. Once you understand that nervousness is natural, and indeed necessary, it becomes a little easier to handle.

Everyone is frightened of the unknown. Any presentation involves an element of uncertainty, because it's 'live'. You can't plan for the audience's mood on the day. You may not even be able to foresee who will be there. You can't plan for any sudden development that affects the proposal or explanation you are giving. You can't plan for every question that you might be asked. This is, of course, the greatest strength of presentations: you and the audience are together, in the same place, at the same time. You are bringing the material alive for them, here and now. If nothing is left to chance, the presentation will remain dead on the floor.

The trick is to know what to leave to chance. If you can support your nerves with solid preparation, you can channel your nervous energy into the performance itself. Prepare well, and you will be ready to bring the presentation to life.

You can prepare in three areas:

1. the material;
2. the audience;
3. yourself.

In each case, preparation means taking control. If you can remove the element of uncertainty in these areas, you will be ready to encounter what can't be controlled: the instantaneous and living relationship between you and your audience.

Managing the material

Many presentations fail, not because the presenter is weak, but because the material is disorderly. The audience tries its utmost to understand, but gets lost. You have to remember that they will forget virtually everything you say. They may remember rather more of what you show them, but only if it is quite simple. Don't expect any audience to remember, from the presentation alone, more than half a dozen ideas.

In presentations, more than in any other kind of corporate communication, you must display the shape of your thinking. That shape will only be clear if you keep it simple. Detail doesn't make things clearer; it makes things more complicated. If you want to display the shape of your thinking, you must design it. Managing the material is a design process (Figure 7.1).

Defining your objective

Why are you making this presentation? That's the first, and most important, question you must answer. Everything else – the material you include, its order, the level of detail you go into,

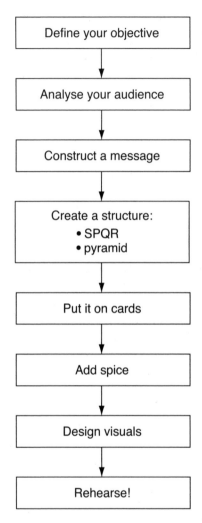

Figure 7.1   Planning a presentation

how long the presentation will last, what visual aids you will use – will depend on your answer to this question.

What do you want your audience to take away at the end of the presentation? More importantly: what do you want them to do? Your objective is to tell them everything they need to know to take that action – and nothing more.

Presentations are not for giving information. To repeat: your audience is probably going to forget almost all the information you give them. So packing the presentation full of information is almost certainly counterproductive. If you must offer your audience detailed information, put it in supporting notes.

I believe that there's only one reason why you should be making a presentation. It may sound rather grand, but a presentation should *inspire* your audience. They want to be interested: to be moved, involved, intrigued. Your task is to bring your ideas alive with your own feelings, commitment and passion. You can

How many points to put across?

I think the answer should be 'one'. If the average member of the audience can remember with interest and enthusiasm one main theme, the lecture has been a great success.

(Sir Lawrence Bragg, quoted in Max Atkinson, *Lend Me Your Ears*, Vermilion Press, London, 2004)

demonstrate this commitment further when the audience asks you questions. It's your conviction that the audience is looking for.

So your objective must be to inspire your audience. If you have any other objective, choose another method of communication. If you are simply making a pronouncement and not seeking or expecting any kind of response, you may as well write it down. For teaching or instructing, you will need to adapt a presentation into a much more interactive activity.

Write your objective down in one sentence. This helps you to:

- clear your mind;
- select material to fit;
- check at the end of planning that you are still addressing a single clear issue.

Write a simple sentence beginning:

'The aim of this presentation is to...'

Make sure the verb following that word 'to' is suitably inspirational!

Analysing your audience

Your presentation will be successful if the audience feels that you have spoken directly to them. If you can demonstrate that you have tailored your material to their needs, the audience will be more inclined to accept it.

So think about your audience carefully

- **How many will there be?**
- **What is their status range?**
- **Will they want to be there?**
- **How much do they already know about the matter? How much more do they need to know?**
- **What will they be expecting? What is the history, the context, the rumour, the gossip?**
- **How does your message and your material relate to the audience? Relevance defines what you will research, include and highlight. It will also help you to decide where to start: what your point of entry will be.**

- Is the audience young or old? Are they predominantly one gender or mixed?
- Are they technical specialists or generalists? They will want different levels of detail.
- Where are they in the organisation? Different working groups will have different interests and different ways of looking at the world.

Think, too, about the audience's expectations of the presentation. They may see presentations often, or very rarely. They may also have specific expectations of you, the presenter: they may know you well or hardly at all; you may have some sort of reputation that goes before you.

Match or exceed your audience's expectations

Broadly, your audience has certain expectations, of you and of itself. How will you meet these, or exceed them? You may, of course, want to confound their expectations: but this may be a little risky!

Audience's expectations of you	Audience's expectations of itself
Set direction and pace	To be led
Be competent	To work at the speaker's pace
Know your stuff	To be told what to do (take notes, ask questions, etc)
Be confident	

Constructing a message

Once you have your objective, and you have some sense of who your audience is, you can begin to plan your material. Begin with a clear message. This should have all the characteristics of the messages that we looked at in Chapter 5. Your message must:

- **be a sentence;**
- **express your objective;**
- **contain a single idea;**
- **have no more than 15 words;**
- **grab your audience's attention.**

You might consider putting this message on to a slide or other visual aid and show it near the start of the presentation. But an effective message should stick in the mind without any help. Make your message as vivid as you can.

Creating a structure

Everything in the structure of the presentation should support your message. Keep the structure of your presentation simple. The audience will forget most of what you say to them. Make sure that they remember your message and a few key points.

Weaving an introduction

Use SPQR to start the presentation, leading the audience from where they are to where you want them to be. This also allows you to show that you understand their situation and that you are there to help them. Using SPQR will convince them that you have put yourself into their shoes. The more obvious the problem is to the audience, the less time you will need to spend on SPQR.

SPQR also allows you to demonstrate your own credentials for being there. (Look back at the notes on *ethos* in Chapter 5.) Your values and beliefs are what make you credible to the audience: remember, they are judging you as well as what you have to say. What qualifies you to speak on this subject? What special experience or expertise do you have? How can you add value to the ideas in your presentation?

Your own values and beliefs will be more credible if you can weave them into a story. SPQR gives you the structure. You could begin your presentation by telling a brief story, making sure that your audience will be able to relate to it. Stories have a way of sticking in the mind long after arguments have faded. Choose a story that demonstrates your values in relation to the matter in hand. Beware generalised sentiment. Avoid 'motherhood and apple pie' stories. Make the story authentic and relevant. And keep it brief. You need to allow as much time as possible for your new ideas.

Building a pyramid

Use a pyramid structure to outline your small number of key points. Show the pyramid visually: overhead or PowerPoint slides, or a flip chart. Indicate that these key points will form the sections of the presentation.

Repetition is an essential feature of good presentations. Because the audience can't reread or rewind to remind themselves of what you said, you need to build their recall by repeating the key features of your presentation. The key features will be your message, your structure, your key points and any call to action that you deliver at the end. Aim to build the audience's recall on no more than about half-a-dozen pieces of information.

Most people seem to know the famous *tell 'em* principle:

- **Tell 'em what you're going to tell 'em.**
- **Tell 'em.**
- **Tell 'em what you've told 'em.**

This valuable technique is one you should use often in your presentation. Build the three-part repetition into the presentation as a whole: tell 'em at the start what the whole presentation will cover; and tell 'em at the end what the whole thing has covered. Use the technique, too, within each part of the presentation: summarising at the start and end, so that you lead the audience into and out of each section explicitly.

Don't be afraid to repeat your ideas. If you want the audience to remember them, you can't repeat them too often.

If you plan well, you will almost certainly create too much material. You must now decide what to leave out, and what you could leave out if necessary. Be ruthless. Bear in mind that your audience will forget most of what you say. Go back to your pyramid and make sure that you have enough time to cover each key point. Weed out any detail that will slow you down or divert you from your objective.

Opening and closing the presentation

Once the body of the presentation is in place, you need to design an opening and close that will help you take off and land safely. You need to be able to perform these on 'autopilot'. Memorise them word for word or write them out in full.

The opening of your presentation should include:

- **introducing yourself – who you are and why you are there;**
- **acknowledging the audience – thanking them for their time and recognising what they are expecting;**
- **a clear statement of your objective or, better still, your message;**
- **a timetable – finish times, breaks if necessary;**
- **rules and regulations – note-taking, how you will take questions;**
- **any 'housekeeping' items – safety, refreshments, administration.**

Once these elements are in place, you can decide exactly how to order the items. You might decide to start with something surprising or unusual: launching into a story or a striking example, seemingly improvising some remark about the venue or immediate circumstances of your talk, asking a question. Sometimes it's a good idea to talk with the audience at the very start before launching into the presentation proper.

The close of the presentation is the most memorable moment. Whatever else happens, the audience will almost certainly remember this! This is your last chance to 'tell 'em what you've told 'em.' Summarise your key points, and your message. Give a call to action. Add feeling: this is the place for you to invoke *pathos*. (Look back at the start of Chapter 5 for more on this.) Be specific in your call to action: what *exactly* do you want the audience to do?

Thank the audience for their attention. You might also formally guide them into a question session, giving them time to relax after concentrating and perhaps pre-arranging a 'planted question' in the audience to set the ball rolling.

Putting it on cards

Put your ideas on to cards. These are useful memory devices and will help you to bring the presentation alive.

The best presentations are given without notes. But few people will always have the confidence or experience to be able to deliver without any help. Nevertheless, any notes you create should aim to support your memory, not substitute for it.

Don't write your presentation out in full unless you are an accomplished actor. Only actors can make recitation sound convincing – and nobody is asking you to act. Use cards. Filing or archive cards are best; use the largest you can find. Cards have a number of key advantages.

- **They are less shaky than paper – they don't rustle.**
- **They are more compact.**
- **They give your hands something firm to hold.**
- **They can be tagged with a treasury tag to prevent loss of order.**
- **They look more professional.**
- **They force you to write only brief notes.**

By writing only brief notes, triggers and cues on your cards, you force yourself to think about what you are saying, while you are saying it. This means that you will sound much more convincing. Obviously, your audience will only tolerate a certain amount of silence while you think of the next thing to say. The note on the card is there to trigger that next point and keep you moving.

Write your notes in bold print, using pen or felt-tip. Write on only one side and number the cards sequentially. Include:

- what you *must* say;
- what you *should* say to support the main idea;
- what you *could* say if you have time.

Add notes on timing, visual aids, cues for your own behaviour. Keep the cards simple to look at and rehearse with them so that you get to know them.

Adding spice

Exciting presentations bring ideas alive. You are the medium through which the audience understands the material. You must make the presentation your own and give it the spicy smell of real life.

Rack your brain for anything you can use. Think it up, cook it up, dream it up if necessary. Look for:

- images;
- examples;
- analogies;
- stories;
- pictures;
- jokes (but be very careful about these).

The aim is to create pictures in your audience's mind. Don't let computer graphics do it all for you. And don't fall into the trap of thinking that putting text on a visual aid makes it visual. Your audience wants *images*: real pictures, not words.

The most powerful pictures are the ones you can conjure up in your audience's imagination with your own words. There's a famous story about a little girl who claimed she liked plays on the radio, 'because the pictures were better'. You should be aiming to create such pictures in your audience's mind.

Designing visuals

Working on the visuals can take longer than any other part of planning. The important thing to remember is that any aid you use is there to help you, not to substitute for you. You are *not* a voice-over accompanying a slide presentation; the pictures are there to illustrate your ideas. The audience wants to see *you*: to meet with you, assess you, ask you questions, learn about you. They will not have the chance to do any of this if you hide behind your visual aids.

Visual aids intrude. The moment you turn on the projector or turn to the flipchart, the audience's attention is on that rather than you. A small number of excellent visual aids will have far more impact than a large number of indifferent ones. Don't fall into the trap of thinking that every part of the presentation should have an accompanying slide.

Make your visuals just that: *visual*. If you can avoid using words, do so. How can you put the information into graphic form? Is there a picture you can use to illustrate or suggest what you are saying? Words are for listening to. Visual aids are for looking at. It really is that simple.

6 × 6 × 6

If you *must* put words on your slides, they should obey this design principle.

No more than six lines of text on any slide.

No more than six words on any one line.

The text should be visible *on a laptop screen* from a distance of six metres. (For most fonts, this means a minimum size of about 24pt.)

Audiences' expectations of slides are changing. We all know that it's quite easy to produce slides with flashy animation. Many people are becoming bored with endless slide shows filled with more or less poorly designed slides. Confound your audience's expectations. Use the technology by all means – and then leap away from it, galvanising your audience with your own passion for your subject. Or be really daring, and work without any slides at all.

Rehearsing

There is a world of difference between thinking your presentation through and doing it. You may think you know what you want to say, but until you say it you don't really know. Only by uttering it aloud can you test whether you understand what you are saying. Rehearsal is the reality check.

Rehearsal is also a time check. Time acts oddly in presentations. It can seem to stop, to drag and – more often than not – to race away. The most common time problem I encounter with trainees who are rehearsing their presentations is that they run out of time. They are astounded when I tell them that time is up and they have hardly finished introducing themselves! You *must* rehearse to see how long it all takes. Be aware that it will probably take longer than you anticipate: maybe 50 per cent longer.

Rehearsing: general guidelines

- Rehearse in real time: don't skip bits.
- Rehearse with a friend. Ask them what they think and work with them to improve.
- Rehearse with your notes. Get into the habit of looking up from them.
- Rehearse with the visual aids at least once.
- Rehearse in the venue itself if you can. If you can't, try to spend some time there, getting the feel of the room.

The ultimate aim of rehearsal is to give you freedom in the presentation itself. Once you have run through the presentation a few times, you will be able to concentrate on the most important element of the event; your relationship with the audience. Under-rehearsed presenters spend too much time working out what to say. Well-rehearsed presenters know what to say and can improvise on it according to the demands of the moment.

Try to think of each presentation as brand new. After all, it's probably new for this particular audience. They haven't heard your stories or arguments before. They are going on this journey for the first time. Change the material a little each time you present. Think of a new story or a new example.

You must also rehearse with any equipment that you intend to use. Nothing is more nerve-wracking than trying to present with a projector or laptop you've never seen before. Rehearse also to improve your use of the equipment:

- **Talk without support. Don't use the visuals as a crib.**
- **Don't talk to visuals. They can't hear you. Avoid turning your back on the audience.**

- Don't let the light of the visuals put you in darkness.
- Make sure you know how to put things right if they go wrong.
- If you can, be ready to present without any visual aids at all.

Controlling the audience

Many presenters concentrate so hard on the material that they ignore the audience. They have no idea of the messages that their body is sending out. They are thinking so hard about *what* they are saying that they have no time to think about *how* they say it.

You are performing. Your whole body is involved. You must become aware of what your body is doing so that you can control it, and thus the audience. A few basic principles will ensure that you keep the audience within your control.

Eye contact

You speak more with your eyes than with your voice. Your eyes tell the audience that you are taking notice of them, that you are confident to speak to them, that you know what you are talking about and that you believe what you are saying.

Look at the audience's eyes throughout the presentation. Imagine that a lighthouse beam is shooting out from your eyes and scanning the audience. Make sure that the beam enters every pair of eyes in the room. Focus for a few seconds on each pair of eyes and meet their gaze. Don't look past them, through them or over their heads. Pick out a few faces that look particularly friendly and return to them. After a while, you may even feel confident enough to return to a few of the less friendly ones!

Include the whole audience with your eyes. Many presenters fall into the trap of focusing on only one person: the most senior manager, the strongest personality, maybe simply someone they like a lot.

Keep your cue cards in your hand so that you can easily glance down at them and bring your eyes back to the audience quickly.

Your face

The rest of your face is important, too! Remember to smile. Animate your face and remember to make everything just a little larger than life so that your face can be 'read' at the back of the room.

Gestures

Many presenters worry about how much or little they gesture. This is reasonable. Arms and hands are prominent parts of the body and can sometimes get out of control.

The important thing is to find the gestures that are natural for you. If you are a great gesticulator, don't try to force your hands into rigid stillness. If you don't normally gesture a great deal, don't force yourself into balletic movements. Use your hands to paint pictures and to help you get the words out. Keep your gestures open, away from your body and into the room. Don't cross your hands behind your back or in front of your crotch, and don't put them in your pockets too much. (It's a good idea to empty your pockets before the presentation so that you don't find yourself jingling coins or keys.)

Movement

Aim for stillness. This doesn't mean that you should stand completely still all the time. Moving about the room shows that you are making the space your own, and helps to energise the space between you and the audience. But rhythmic, repetitive movement can be annoying and suggest the neurotic pacing of a panther in a cage. Try not to rock on your feet or tie your legs in knots! Aim to have both feet on the ground as much as possible and slow down your movements.

It can sometimes help to sit to present. You might practise with a chair, or the back of a chair, a stool or even the edge of a table. Make sure that it is stable and solid enough to bear your weight!

Looking after yourself

And you will *still* be nervous as the moment of truth approaches. Remember that those nerves are there to help you. If you have prepared adequately, you should be ready to use them to encounter the uncertainty of live performance.

You certainly need time before presenting that is quiet and focused. I need to spend about 15 minutes doing nothing but preparing myself mentally. I put myself where nothing can distract me from the presentation. Visualising success immediately before the presentation works for some people. Ahead of time, imagine yourself presenting, the audience attentively listening to your every word, applauding you at the end and asking keen questions afterwards.

On some occasions it can be useful to meet the audience and chat with them before you start. This can break the ice and put you more at ease. In truth, I rarely feel comfortable doing this; for others, it can be highly beneficial in relaxing them and preparing for the presentation.

The most important preparation involves breathing. Make contact with the deepest kind of breathing, which works from the stomach rather than the upper part of the lungs. Slow that breathing down, and make it calm, regular and strong. This works wonders for the voice: it gives it depth and power, and makes for a more convincing delivery.

Along with your breathing, pay attention to the muscles around your mouth that help you to articulate. Try some tongue-twisters or sing a favourite song. Chew the cud, and get your tongue and lips really working and warmed up. A very simple exercise is to stick your tongue as far out of your mouth as you can and then speak a part of your presentation, trying to make the consonants as clear as you can. You only need to do this for about 30 seconds to wake up your voice and make it clearer. You will, of course, look rather silly while doing this, so it's best to do the exercise in a private place!

Answering questions

Many presenters are as worried about the question session as about the presentation itself. A few guidelines can help to turn your question session from a trial into a triumph:

- *Decide when to take questions.* **This will probably be at the end. But you might prefer to take questions during the presentation. This is more difficult to manage but can improve your relationship with the audience.**
- *Anticipate the most likely questions.* **These may be 'Frequently Asked Questions' that you can easily foresee. Others may arise from the particular circumstances of the presentation.**
- *Use a 'plant'.* **Ask somebody to be ready with a question to start the session off. Audiences are sometimes hesitant at the end of a presentation about breaking the atmosphere.**
- *Answer concisely.* **Force yourself to be brief.**
- *Answer honestly.* **You can withhold information, but don't lie. Someone in the audience will almost certainly see through you.**
- *Take questions from the whole audience.* **From all parts of the room and from different 'social areas'.**
- *Answer the whole audience.* **Don't let questions seduce you into private conversations. Make sure the audience has heard the question.**

• *If you don't know, say so.* And promise what you'll do to answer later.

A simple format for answering a question

- Repeat the question if necessary. This helps you understand it, helps the audience to hear it, and gives you time to think about your answer.
- Give a single answer. Make only one point.
- Now give one reason for your answer.
- Give an example that illustrates the point.

Of course, it may not be easy to think of all these as you spontaneously respond to a question. But if you slow down and try to think this simple format through, you will probably answer more succinctly and clearly.

8

Putting it in writing

Writing well is probably the most technically difficult form of communication. It requires skill, understanding and a good deal of creativity. And we are judged on the quality of our writing. It has to act as our ambassador in our absence.

We all know effective writing when we see it. It does its job clearly and quickly. It says what the writer wants to say; nothing gets in the way. Above all, effective writing gets results.

Writing for results

Whenever we write a business document, we are seeking a result. That's why I prefer the term 'functional writing' to 'business writing'. Functional writing has a job to do. It has a practical purpose.

Writing well starts with choosing to write. You don't need to achieve your purpose by writing. Writing is slow and expensive; even writing an e-mail can take time. A telephone call may do the job more quickly. Writing is useful when:

- you want a permanent record;
- the information is complicated; or
- you want to copy the same material to many readers.

It may be useful to write to someone who is never available to talk to, though there is no guarantee that they will read your message among the dozens or hundreds they receive that day. Writing also carries a certain authority that a conversation may lack. A letter may get action more easily than a phone call because it looks more serious or official.

Making reading easier

Most of the advantages of conversation disappear when we write. Compared to talking and listening, writing and reading are slow and inefficient. A document isn't dynamic; it's static. Misunderstandings can easily arise. If the reader gets something wrong, you aren't there to help out. Worst of all, you can't even be sure that the reader will read the document.

Good writers try to make reading as easy as possible. Reading, after all, is hard work. We read on three levels:

- working out what the writer has to say;
- scanning sentences for complete ideas;
- reading individual words for their meaning.

To make reading easier, you must help the reader on all three levels.

The three golden rules of writing
- Use words that the reader is most likely to understand.
- Construct straightforward sentences.
- Make your point, then support it.

Generally, short words are easier to understand than long ones. But your reader will understand best the words that are *familiar* to them. If they know the jargon or the long abstract words, use them. If in doubt, use short words.

Similarly, shorter sentences are clearer than longer ones. But a page full of short sentences will have a 'scatter-gun' effect: lots of points but no connections. Sentences also work best when they are well constructed and grouped together in paragraphs.

The final golden rule is the most important. Many of us write in a kind of 'stream of consciousness', putting one idea after another until we reach our conclusion. This gives our writing flow. But we should also be distinct, making sure that our ideas leap out at the reader and hook their attention. If you have something to say, always aim to say it as soon as possible. Then deliver the evidence that supports your idea.

Writing step by step

Writing is best tackled systematically. We all face the temptation to do everything at once: working out what to say, in what order, and how to say it. This is a recipe for disaster: we get confused and frustrated and the writing that emerges is a garbled mess. Like cooking, writing is best done step by step.

Think in terms of constructing a document rather than merely writing it. This letter or document has a job to do; you must design and build it to do the job. The construction process has three steps:

- **designing the document;**
- **writing a first draft;**
- **editing the draft.**

Try to keep the stages separate. If you can take breaks between them, so much the better. It can also be useful to ask a colleague for help at each stage.

In this chapter, we look at these three stages and explore the key issues in each. Many of the techniques will already be familiar to you. The idea of delivering a single message, SPQR (situation–problem–question–response) and using a pyramid structure for organising information, all have a place in writing well.

Designing the document

We can break planning a document into five stages:

- **goal orientation;**
- **readership analysis;**
- **creating a message;**
- **organising information;**
- **constructing an outline.**

Goal orientation

Start by identifying the purpose of your document. Distinguish between the document's purpose and its subject. Whatever you are writing about, you must be clear what you want to achieve.

Make your purpose as specific as possible. Take care not to create a purpose that is inappropriate. For example, documents cannot analyse or evaluate. These are thinking processes. The document will display the product of your thinking. It can't do the thinking!

What do you want the document to do?

Try these verbs out for size.

I want this document to

recommend	identify	respond
notify	update	summarise
announce	confirm	describe
clarify	invite	propose
compare	justify	request
explain	argue	suggest
highlight	outline	categorise

What do you want the reader to do as a result of reading the document? Functional documents demand action and deliver information to help achieve it. Identify the action you want the reader to take and you will be better placed to provide the information that will help them take it.

What do you want the reader to do?

Here are some suggestions.

I want the reader to

target areas for action	realign strategy
attend a meeting	approve funding
implement plan	answer questions
provide input	complete a task
agree with me	review my proposal
choose from options	give me feedback
put something right	investigate an issue

Formalise your objective into a **function statement**. If necessary, agree this with the document's 'client', the person who has asked for it. By agreeing the document's functions, you will know exactly what is required of you.

Function statement

I want this document to

[immediate aim]

so that

[proposed action]

Readership analysis

Your document may circulate to a wide readership. Different readers will have different expectations, priorities and levels of knowledge. Analyse the readership so that you can organise information in the document more effectively.

Managing readership expectations

Categorise your readership into **primary, secondary** and **tertiary** readers. The primary readership must read the document. The document is designed for them. The secondary readership may look at only part of the document. It may include your manager, who may need to authorise it before circulation but who will not act on it. The tertiary readership may include people you will never meet but who may use the document in some unforeseen way. You will need to satisfy all of these readers. But you must design the document for the primary readership alone.

Identifying the key persuasive factors

The key persuasive factors are the most important elements in your reader's decision to believe you. They may arise from the reader's:

- **background;**
- **priorities;**
- **needs or concerns;**
- **place in the corporate culture;**
- **relationship to the external environment.**

Put yourself in the primary reader's position and ask: 'What would most convince me about this idea?'

Creating a message

Your document must deliver a single message.

The message is the most important element of the document. Everything else in it – the material, how it is ordered, how you present it – depends on the message.

The message is the single most important point you want to make to the reader to express your objective. It is not a heading or title. Neither is it a description of what you are doing in the document. The message *expresses* your purpose. Your document's message should be:

- **a sentence;**
- **expressing a single idea;**
- **no longer than 15 words long; that is**
- **self-explanatory to the reader;**
- **action-centred.**

It is critically important to check that your document's message is appropriate: to you, to the reader, and to your material. In a conversation, interview or presentation, we can check that we are addressing the other person's needs, or the audience's expectations, on the spot. When we write, that interaction disappears. Many documents fail to give their readers what they want. SPQR is the only way you can check that you are producing the document that the reader will find useful.

Look back at Chapter 5 for more details about SPQR. The SPQR sequence can:

- **help you validate your message;**
- **facilitate a conversation between writer and reader to clarify the document's message;**
- **form the core of an Introduction in the document.**

Organising information

In writing, more than anywhere else, communicating well is a matter of displaying the shape of your thinking. That shape is made up of ideas: the sentences you write. You must arrange those ideas into a coherent shape that the reader can see clearly.

Your reader can understand only one piece of information clearly at a time. To understand your message in more detail, they must first break it into pieces, then understand each piece in order. You must organise information, therefore, in two dimensions:

- **vertically (breaking the message into pieces, grouping smaller pieces into larger ones);**
- **horizontally (organising each group of pieces into an order).**

Organising information like this creates a shape that allows the reader's mind to understand complexity in the most natural way. The shape you create is a pyramid.

First- and second-stage thinking

We can imagine the process of creating the document's structure as a thinking process in two stages. We have looked at the two stages of thinking already as a way of structuring our conversations (Chapter 3). Now we can use them to help us organise material for a document:

- *first-stage thinking:* gathering information;
- *second-stage thinking:* organising the information.

Use mindmaps to help you gather information, and the pyramid principle to help you organise it into a coherent structure.

Summarising and grouping

Imagine speaking your message to the reader. What question will it provoke in their mind? The question should be one of three:

- 'Why?'
- 'How?'
- 'Which ones?'

You must have at least two answers to the question. Try to have no more than six. Write your answers to that question as key points. All your key points must be sentences. You should be able to align each key point to a group of ideas on your mindmap.

Creating key points

Your key points should all be of the same kind.

• 'Why?'	Reasons, benefits, causes
• 'How?'	Procedures, process steps
• 'Which ones?'	Items, categories, factors

For each key point, ask what question it provokes: 'Why?', 'How?' or 'Which ones?' Identify the answers to that question and write these as sub-points. Repeat if necessary for each sub-point to create minor points. For every question, you must have more than one answer.

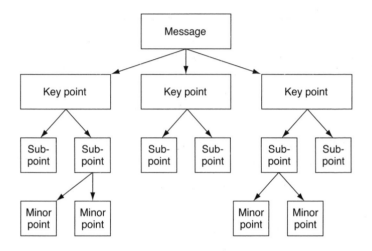

Figure 8.1   Building a pyramid

Building the pyramid

The result of this question-and-answer process is a pyramid structure (Figure 8.1).

Building pyramids: essential principles

- Every idea must be a sentence.
- Each idea must summarise the ideas grouped beneath it.
- Each idea within a group is an answer to the question provoked by the summarising idea.

Managing detail

Building a pyramid creates a discipline that allows you to work out how much information to include in your document and how to order it.

Pyramid building always proceeds by division. Each idea provokes a question to which you must have at least two answers – and preferably not more than six. This process of division by question and answer continues until an idea fails to provoke a question with multiple answers. It can stop if:

- **an idea does not provoke a question from the reader;**
- **an idea provokes a question that has only one answer.**

It should never be necessary to create a pyramid containing more than four levels: message, key point, sub-point, minor point.

You must decide how to order ideas in each group. You can order ideas in terms of:

- **rank (size, importance, priority, relevance);**
- **process steps;**
- **chronology;**
- **logical reasoning.**

Sometimes the order of ideas is not critical.

Constructing an outline

The final stage of planning your document is constructing an outline. This transforms your pyramid into text that you can expand into a first draft.

An outline is the design of your document. It gives an overview of the entire document in miniature. Here's how to write an outline.

- At the top of a page, write your message sentence, headed *Message*.
- Follow this with a headed *Introduction*: SPQR, briefly stated (three or four lines at most).
- Write each key point sentence, numbered, in order, with each sub-point and minor point numbered beneath each key point. Use a decimal numbering system for maximum clarity:
  - *1.*
  - *1.1*
  - *1.1.1* and so on.
- Add a title for the whole outline, and headings for each key point, if necessary.

Once you understand this principle of creating an outline, you can adapt it to any kind of document. We'll look here at three basic formats: e-mail or memo, letter and report. You'll see that the pyramid remains the same in each case, with only slight variations.

Outlining an e-mail or memo

This is the simplest kind of pyramid.

Simply place your message at the top, immediately after your salutation. Create a short paragraph – or even a simple bullet point – for each key point and end, if necessary, with a call to action: the next step you want the reader to take.

It's an excellent idea to compress your message into the subject line of the e-mail so that it appears on the reader's inbox menu.

E-mail has become a standard mode of communicating in organisations. It's fast, cheap and easy to use. But in many organisations, e-mail is rapidly becoming the problem rather than the solution. Four factors seem to be contributing to this impending crisis:

- *Information overload.* A recent survey suggested that managers receive an average of 178 e-mails a day. Getting yours noticed may be the biggest problem in getting it read.
- *Death of the conversation.* Many of us now hardly talk to each other; we send e-mails instead. As a result, e-mail is becoming infected with substitutes for social contact. Lonely cubicle workers spread gossip in private jargon, spiced with 'emoticons' and cryptic symbols.
- *More haste, less understanding.* The style of writing in e-mail is becoming relaxed to the point of garbled.
- *Overflowing inboxes.* When was the last time you weeded your inbox?

E-mail is writing. Treat it as you would any other kind of writing. Plan, write, edit. Here are 10 more tips to help e-mail work better for you:

1. **Make your message clear.**
2. **Minimise information.** Don't make the reader scroll down.
3. **Put the message in the subject line.** It's much more useful to have a headline-style message in this line than a heading.
4. **Don't shout.** Avoid capital letters, underlining and bold. Above all, avoid facetious or all-purpose headings such as 'Urgent' or 'Read this now!'
5. **Don't fan 'flames'.** Don't write anything in an e-mail that you wouldn't say face to face.
6. **Avoid emoticons.** Don't use symbols or silly abbreviations. Use English.
7. **Edit before sending.** E-mail is so fast that you can easily spend a few moments checking sense, spelling and punctuation.
8. **Remember that e-mail is public.** Most e-mail can be accessed on central servers. Never write anything that a lawyer might use against you.

9. **Don't spam.** Send only messages that you must send, to the individuals who need to read them. Avoid blanket copies.
10. **Clear your inbox regularly.** You'll make the system – and yourself – work much more efficiently.

Outline of an e-mail

Re: conference meeting, 2 April: key issues

Derek
There are three key issues I'd like to discuss at our meeting on Friday.

- How can we promote the conference more effectively abroad?
- How can we align the main speakers' messages effectively to support corporate strategy?
- Do we have the resources to create an informal exhibition area in the foyer?

If you have any other issues to raise, copy me in. See you there!
Gloria

Outlining a letter

The pyramid here is framed by handshakes: one at the start, and possibly one at the end. The style of a letter may differ slightly from that of an e-mail (more on style later), but apart from that, and a few other formalities of layout, the two are similar.

Outline of a letter

25 January 2010   [company logo]
Sidney Reader
Readership House
READERTOWN
AB1 2CD

Dear Sidney

Thank you for your letter of 20 January.   [*handshake*]

This is my main message.   [*message sentence*]

My first point is here.   [*paragraphs*]

...

My second point is here.

...

The next step is   [*action point*]

I hope this is satisfactory.   [*closing handshake*]

Yours sincerely

Alan Writer
[Job title]

Outlining a report

Reports tend to need the fullest kind of outline, complete with summary, introduction, numbered points and an array of sub-points and minor points.

Creating the outline is a really useful stage in constructing a report. You can use the outline to check with the report's 'client' that it is developing as they would wish, to make changes to your report without having to rewrite lots of text, and to establish that you know exactly what your key ideas are for each section. The outline can itself form the summary of the report. It will also be invaluable for those readers who only want reports that cover a single sheet of A4. For them, the outline *is* the report.

Outline of a report

Message
We should locate new plant in Gatheringham.

Introduction
Our business is rapidly expanding. Existing manufacturing plant will reach capacity within three years. We urgently need to decide where to locate new manufacturing plant. This document summarises the findings of the relocation project and justifies its recommendation in strategic terms.

1. Capital costs in Gatheringham are estimated at 10 per cent below those of the next best location.
   1.1 Constructors' bids in the area average 10 per cent below those in other locations.
   1.2 Land costs are on average 13 per cent lower than in other areas.
2. Operating costs in Gatheringham are estimated to be 15 per cent lower than in other areas.
   2.1 Labour costs are 7 per cent less than the national average.
   2.2 Overheads are estimated at 9 per cent less than in current plants.
   2.3 Tax incentives for operating in this zone are very attractive.

3. Distribution costs would decrease by at least 7 per cent if centred on Gatheringham.

   3.1 The area is centrally located for our markets.

   3.2 The local infrastructure is well developed.

Writing a first draft

Writing the document should be considerably easier now that the outline is complete. Essentially, you need to expand the outline by adding text, headings, and – for reports in particular – numbering and graphics. The plan of the outline is in place, and the sentences in the outline give you a clear idea of what you want to say in each paragraph and section.

Think of writing the first draft of your document as a separate activity from either planning or editing.

- *Write quickly.* **Don't ponder over words. Keep going. Leave gaps if necessary. Aim for a natural flow.**
- *Write in your own voice.* **Expressing yourself in your own way will help you to say what you mean more exactly. If your reader can 'hear' your voice, reading will be easier.**
- *Write without interruption.* **Try to find a time and place where you can think and write without distractions.**
- *Write without editing.* **Don't try to get it right first time. Resist the temptation to edit as you go. You will tend to get stuck and waste time.**
- *Keep to the plan of your outline.* **Use the sentences from your outline to focus what you want to say. If you find yourself wandering from the point, stop and move on to the next sentence in the outline.**

Navigation aids

Effective documents contain navigation aids to help the reader find their way around. The most important of these are:

- **summaries;**
- **introductions;**
- **headings;**
- **bullet points.**

All of these elements will help you 'sell' the document to your reader.

Summaries and introductions

Don't confuse these two essential items.

The **summary** is the document in miniature. At its heart is your message. Place the summary at the very start of the document – immediately following the title page. Your outline is a ready-made summary.

An **introduction** explains how the document came into being. At its heart is SPQR: background information including the problem addressed by the document and the question it answers. Introductions might expand to include:

- **methodology;**
- **acknowledgements;**
- **a short guide to the document, section by section.**

Use summaries elsewhere in the document to deliver the shape of the material – most importantly, at the start of each section.

Headings

Pay close attention to the title and other headings in your document. They should have high scanning value: the reader should be able to glean a lot of information from relatively few words. 'Financial review', for example, has low scanning value. 'Breakdown of operating costs 2006' works rather better.

Headings should be informative without being too detailed. In a report, you might assemble your headings into a contents list. Check it to see that the headings give a fair idea of content and are not too repetitious.

Bullet points

Bullet points are visually very powerful. There is a danger, therefore, that you can use them too much. Don't overuse them.

- **Construct the points in parallel. All items should be grammatically of the same kind.**
- **Make the points consistent with the 'platform': the text that introduces the list.**
- **Improve the 'platform' so that repeated elements in the list need be expressed only once.**

Effective editing

The aim of editing is to make the first draft easier to read.

Editing is about making choices. It is potentially endless because there is never only one way to say what you mean. It's especially difficult to edit your own work. Ask a colleague to help you if you can. Try to cultivate an innocent eye. Take a break before editing so that you are better prepared to look at the text afresh.

Edit systematically. Editing word by word is time-consuming and may be counterproductive. To edit efficiently, work on three separate levels in this order:

- **paragraphs;**
- **sentences;**
- **words.**

It's probably best to edit hard copy, rather than on screen.

Creating effective paragraphs

Paragraphs display the shape of your thinking. They show the individual main ideas and the relationships between them. Every time you take a step, alter your point of view or change direction, you should start a new paragraph.

Use a topic sentence at the start of each paragraph to summarise it. Topic sentences help you to decide what to include in each paragraph. You can think of a topic sentence as the paragraph's message. It should:

- **be a fully grammatical sentence;**
- **make a single point;**
- **contain no more than 15 words;**
- **say something new.**

An outline, of course, is a ready source of topic sentences. Another place to look for potential topic sentences is at the end of a paragraph. Very often we put the most important idea as the paragraph's conclusion. Try flipping that conclusion to the start of the paragraph as a topic sentence. Topic sentences should make sense in order. You should be able to read all the topic sentences and understand a section in summary.

Editing a paragraph

To minimise potential downtime and operational risk, it is recommended that the business case for the purchase of a back-up server, which could also be used for system testing, be formally examined. We are now addressing this since a decision is needed by the end of March to avoid additional hire costs or the loss of the rented machine.

Note how a topic sentence allows the writer to cut down the paragraph considerably and improve readability.

We are now examining the business case for buying a back-up server. This could:

- *minimise potential down-time;*
- *minimise operational risk;*
- *also be used for system testing.*

A decision is needed by the end of March to avoid extra hire costs or the loss of the rented machine.

Sentence construction

Sentences express ideas. They will express your ideas more strongly if they are constructed sturdily. Sentences are weaker when they are too long or poorly built. Aim always in your sentences to say what you mean *and no more*.

Follow the '15–25' rule. Message sentences, topic sentences and other sentences expressing big ideas should never exceed 15 words. All other sentences should remain within 25 words long.

Strengthen sentences by:

- **cutting long sentences into separate sentences;**
- **separating multiple sentences;**
- **rebuilding complicated sentences;**
- **making non-sentences grammatically correct;**
- **finding strong subjects and verbs.**

Editing a long sentence

It was originally planned that data conversion and implementation across the remaining business areas would follow at the end of September 2008, but following a variety of problems, considerable scope drift, changes of personnel on the project team and several amendments to the timetable, conversion did not take place until 1 April 2009 and some users were still using parts of the old system until it was finally disconnected in July 2009.

This is easily improved by cutting the sentence at the conjunctions – but, and – and using a vertical list:

The project team originally planned to convert data and implement the system in remaining business areas at the end of September 2008. However, conversion was delayed by changes in:

- *the scope of the project;*
- *personnel on the project team;*
- *the timetable.*

The system was finally converted on 1 April 2009. Some users continued to use parts of the old system until it was disconnected in July 2009.

Editing words

English has a huge vocabulary. One of the main reasons is that the language is a hybrid; many ideas can be expressed with two or three words. Maybe for this reason more than any other, plain English has grown up as a way of helping us to choose the best words for our needs.

Plain English helps any reader to understand at first reading. It tells the truth without embellishment. It is a code of practice, not a set of rigid rules.

Plain English: essential guidelines

- Make your average sentence length 15 to 20 words.
- Use only the words that your reader is most likely to understand.
- Use only as many words as you need.
- Use the strongest, clearest and most specific verbs you can.
- Say what you mean. Be positive; avoid standard expressions and tired formulas.
- Punctuate clearly and simply.

Managing vocabulary

Certain words cause particular problems with readability. Pay attention in particular to:

- **passive verbs;**
- **abstract nouns;**
- **unnecessary words.**

Passive verbs

Verbs can be either active or passive. An active verb expresses what its subject does; a passive verb expresses what its subject suffers. Sentences with active verbs are shorter, stronger and more dynamic than those with passive ones.

*It is **anticipated** that additional disk space **may** be needed.*

We anticipate that the system will need additional disk space.

Abstract nouns

Nouns name things, people, times, places or qualities. **Concrete nouns** name things physically present in the world (*table, woman, pen, car, tree*); **abstract nouns** name ideas, concepts or qualities that cannot be sensed physically (*growth, awareness, training, marketing, possibility*).

Try to cut down your use of abstract nouns. Replace them, if you can, with verbs or adjectives. If you can replace an abstract noun only with a group of shorter, more concrete words, consider keeping it.

*There were some **differences in configuration** between the two machines which added a **degree** of **complexity** to the exercise.*

The two machines were configured differently, making the exercise more complex.

Unnecessary words

Some words contribute nothing to meaning. You might use them because they sound good, or because you don't know what to say next. Remove them.

The benefits of this arrangement are a saving in consultancy costs and the opportunity for new users to learn the system in a meaningful situation at the same time as they learn their jobs.

This arrangement saves consultancy costs and allows new users to learn the system as part of on-the-job learning.

Developing a readable style

Good writing comes alive in your mind. Nothing comes between the writer and your understanding. Effective writing is transparent.

Bringing your own writing to life is a long-term project. Here are some guidelines to point you in the right direction:

- **say what you mean;**
- **be specific;**
- **be positive;**
- **remove blockages.**

Style is personal. Choosing how to write is like choosing how to dress. Improving your style is not unlike improving your dress sense. Look around; imitate what you admire; aim for functional elegance rather than excessive flamboyance.

Say what you mean

Concentrate on what you want to say, not how to say it. Imagine the reader's response. If you only had a few seconds to get your point across, what would you say? Be sincere, and avoid 'scaffolding': any writing that refers to the fact that you are writing ('In this report, I shall...').

Be specific

Aim to be precise rather than vague. Avoid generalising. Use numbers, and names, so that your writing becomes more personal. Use verbs with a specific meaning and avoid verbs that don't mean much (*get, carry out, perform, give, conduct, implement, move, do*). Make it concrete. Give real examples. And use jargon carefully.

Be positive

The best functional writing is forward-looking and action-centred. Avoid writing too much about what has happened, what hasn't happened, what should have happened or what is wrong. Instead, write about proposals, future action and what you are doing. Make definite promises and avoid emotive language.

Remove blockages

Good writing flows like water in a pipe. The words should be under pressure. Remove blockages so that the meaning flows freely. Wherever you can, transform passive verbs into active ones, and abstract nouns into concrete ones. Remove unnecessary words and exterminate clichés. Punctuate inflated language and connect your sentences together carefully.

Writing for the web

Writing for the web is in many ways like writing for any other medium. A number of key features, however, make reading on screen a different experience from reading on paper. Understanding those features will help you produce more usable text for websites and web-based documents.

Key qualities of web text

Research suggests that web users feel happiest when web text is concise, scannable and objective. 'Concise' means that the text says what it needs to say and no more. 'Scannable' means that big ideas are prominent; that paragraphs are not too long; and that key words are easy to pick out. 'Objective' means that the writer tends to remove their own feelings from the text. Readers want information when they are using the web; opinions and feelings tend to get in the way.

Additionally, readers have voted for:

- **clear navigation aids;**
- **evidence of the writer's credibility; and**
- **an informal style.**

Thinking about your readers

The key to effective web-writing is to think of your reader as a visitor, rather than a long-term associate. Reading a book or a report requires a level of commitment from your reader that web reading simply doesn't demand.

Different types of visitors want different things from the web pages they visit.

- *Viewers* **stay on the page for no more than a few seconds.**
- *Users* **want to do something (such as buying a product or registering for a web community) or find practical information.**
- *Readers* **are willing to browse – and actually read what they find.**

Designing and writing web pages is a matter of satisfying as many of these types of visitor as you can. It's worth remembering a slogan invented by one enterprising web-writer: **'shut the door, they're coming over the fence'.** In other words, visitors to your page could be coming from anywhere: a home page, a search engine, or a link from another page in a completely different part of cyberspace.

Chunking and stacking

Chunk and stack your material to satisfy the needs of viewers, users and readers. Chunking and stacking is a variation on summarising and grouping, the structural technique discussed earlier in this chapter.

- **Chunking means breaking information into manageable, screen-sized pieces.**
- **Stacking means grouping the chunks into categories.**

Chunking and stacking effectively layers the material so that readers can see everything that is on the site easily and also go into as much detail as they want.

Additionally, most web pages will benefit from these features.

- *Create a heading* that tells you where you are at once.
- *Write a message sentence.* We've met messages before – and this message is just like the messages you can create in any other document.
- *Provide supporting information* in fewer than 100 words per paragraph.
- *Create hyperlinks* to other pages. No page should be without a hyperlink to take you somewhere else – even if it's only back to the front page or home page.

Cues for action

Cues for action keep viewers from running away, help users to do what they want to do, and encourage readers to explore the page further.

There are various actions you might want your reader to take. For example, you might want them to:

- **search for information;**
- **contribute to a discussion forum;**
- **buy something;**
- **contact someone;**
- **move to another page.**

Explain explicitly what action readers can take. Whatever you want them to do, make sure that you keep the action simple: as few clicks as possible, with the most basic instructions.

Always write as if you are talking directly to readers, using the word 'you'. And provide an incentive for taking the action. The incentive doesn't have to be financial! Simply telling readers what information they can expect to find by taking the action may be enough.

Cues for action: a few ideas

Click <u>here</u> to find out more about Malaysian bug creepers.

Fill out this <u>form</u> for regular updates on Paradise Project activities.

For help with elderly or disabled visitors, <u>send</u> us your telephone number and we'll contact you 24 hours before your arrival to discuss your requirements.

Take part in our northern tundra <u>quiz</u> and play for some great prizes!

You can make a difference. Sign our <u>petition</u> to save the Mexican fly-eating orchid.

Hyperlinks

Hyperlinks are a powerful innovation in web writing. Unlike conventional headings, they perform two functions: helping the reader to find their way around and acting as the transport to get them there. Hyperlinks might be:

- **keywords in the text;**
- **names in the text; or**
- **instructions: 'Go to the semi-tropical zone'.**

Headings are the most important candidates for hyperlinks. They should act like departure and arrival signs in an airport – telling readers where to go and announcing when they have arrived.

Hyperlinks can often use blurb to give just a little detail of what the heading is promising – and encouraging the reader to go there.

Hyperlinks: some wording ideas

Plants in myth and folklore
Discover some of the world's strangest tales about trees
and flowers

Eco-engineering
How technology can help and hinder conservation

The making of garden flowers
How breeders created our favourite blooms

Making it brief

Once you have made your web pages scannable and objective,
you need to make them brief. Work at three levels: paragraph,
sentence and word.

Keep a complete piece of text within one screen. Summarise,
create short paragraphs of no more than about 100 words, and
use topic sentences – maybe in bold – at the start of each
paragraph, to act as scannable summaries.

Use lists wherever you can. They can of course be lists of
hyperlinks to help readers navigate more easily.

Sentence construction is as important as sentence length.
Make sure that your sentences are as simple as you can make
them: avoid complicated clusters of ideas, passive verbs, and
redundant expressions. Generally, try to keep your sentence
length to no more than 25 words or about two lines of text.

Always write in standard plain English. You're writing for a
global audience. Avoid marketing hype, promotional jargon and
the language of advertising.

Making it look good

Keep the visual elements of your document simple. Use a designer if you can.

Make your print readable. Sans serif fonts (such as Arial, Verdana, Tahoma or Univers) are generally easier to read on screen. Use at least 12pt font and higher if possible.

Avoid too much highlighting (and never use underlining except for links). Don't use too many colours (and never use blue, red or purple except for links). And create columns no more than half a screen width. They are easier to scan than text that spreads the full width of the screen.

Transforming conventional documents into web pages

Sometimes, you will want to put traditionally produced documents onto a website as archive documents. Take the opportunity to make them 'web-friendly'. A few simple design features can make all the difference.

Create a summary at the head of the document – no longer than half a screen long. List the section headings at the head of the document. Create links within the document. Obvious candidates for links are the headings in your list at the top of the document. Another useful link is a permanent link to the top of the document. Make the title and main headings visible within the opening screen – not just on the opening printed page.

9

Networking: the new conversation

Networking is a new name for an old idea. The word may cause us to cringe; but, increasingly, many of us recognise that networking is an essential part of business. A survey by Common Purpose in 2008 found that 68 per cent of business leaders expected their networking activity to increase over the next five years. The number rose to 75 per cent among the younger business leaders, between 25 and 44 years old.

Perhaps the word has a bad reputation because people misunderstand what networking is – or should be. Networking is *not*:

- **selling;**
- **using other people for your own gain; or**
- **putting people on the spot.**

Effective networkers understand that none of us can accomplish our goals alone; that we need others to fulfil our ambitions and dreams. We are all part of communities that contribute to our well-being. Networking is a tool to help us create those communities.

> **Networking is the art of building and sustaining mutually beneficial relationships.**

It's through the relationships we build that we reap the benefits of networking. We can find new resources and new information; we can find help in moving forward in our career. We can find new ways to make a contribution.

Networking can be strategic or spontaneous. Strategic networking is planned; spontaneous networking happens by chance. At its best, strategic networking prepares us for the spontaneous moments of discovery.

To network or not to network?

Networking is both a very old idea and a very new one. John Donne wrote 'No man is an island' in 1624; but the language of social networking has only begun to appear in the last 60 years or so. According to the *Oxford English Dictionary*, the word 'network' – meaning an interconnected group of people – first appeared in 1946. The words 'networker' and 'networking', referring to the activities of such groups, don't appear in print until 1976.

In 1980, Mary-Scott Welch published *Networking: The Great New Way for Women to Get Ahead*. Written, according to her obituary in *The New York Times*, 'in an era when more women were competing for jobs traditionally dominated by men', *Networking* also included the first recorded use of the word 'network' as a verb: 'this book', wrote Ms Welch, 'will show you how to network'.

Networking as a business activity was thus associated from the start with feminism. Perhaps its development is associated with a less masculine, less individualist, approach to business, in which co-operation takes precedence over competition.

What makes networking effective

Effective networking relies on three key qualities: an 'abundance mentality'; generosity; and reciprocity.

Abundance. People with a 'scarcity mentality' have difficulty sharing, because they feel that holding on to their resources – property, knowledge, relationships – is vital to their success. People with an 'abundance mentality' understand that human resources – knowledge, intelligence, imagination – produce more when they are shared.

Scarcity and abundance

Scarcity mentality
- Victory means success at someone else's expense.
- Someone else's success means we have missed an opportunity.
- There are two ways to do it: my way, and your way. My way is the right way.
- Everyone is out for themselves.

Abundance mentality
- Victory means success bringing mutual benefits to all.
- The possibilities of growth and development are unlimited and common to all.
- There are three ways of doing it: my way, your way, and a better way.
- Everyone has something unique to offer.

An 'abundance mentality' needs to be cultivated. We have to work at it. It's easy to slip into the scarcity mentality. Developing an abundance mentality means sacrificing something of our own: power, security, certainty. But the benefits are enormous: an abundance mentality can make us less fearful and more confident.

Generosity. With an abundance mentality, we find it easier to give unconditionally. We can give attention to others; and, as we have seen in Chapter 4, attention is at the heart of effective listening. We can also give information more easily and less egotistically.

Reciprocity. Reciprocity is the recognition that none of us can survive without the help of others. All human relationships are based on the idea of give and take; networking depends for its success critically on reciprocity. Humans seem to be 'hard-wired' for reciprocity; if I give you something, you will almost certainly feel obliged to offer me something in return. Because human achievements rely on co-operation, we need to find ways of trusting each other; and reciprocity provides the currency of trust. My gift to you demonstrates that you can trust me, and is an invitation to you to offer something in return, so that I can begin to trust you.

Preparing to network

As with any other communication skill, strategic networking tends to work better when we are well prepared. Effective networkers know why they are at a networking event. They know what they want to achieve. Networking can be exhausting, so having a plan will help you evaluate your success and decide when you can take a rest.

Preparing yourself

Networking puts us on the spot. However politely we skirt around the subject, the first thing we want to know about someone is who they are: not just a name, but an identity. We are looking for something we can relate to, something we can recognise and feel comfortable with. Whether we are the first to offer the information, or the first to enquire, it helps if we have a clear 'script' that we can draw on to present ourselves clearly and easily to others.

Build your brand

Our brand is what others know us to be. It is not our personality, or our mission in life. It's closer to reputation, but more immediate. Our brand is the message we want to give others about ourselves.

Think of your brand as sitting 'on the surface'. Other qualities sit below the surface: your beliefs, values, attitudes. You don't need to display them, you may not want to display them, and it may be inappropriate to display them. But your brand suggests them.

Finding your core values

1. What matters to you?
2. If you didn't have to work, what would you do?
3. What puts you 'in the zone'?
4. What big problems would you like to do something about?
5. What do you admire in others?
6. What would you like people to say about you at your 75th birthday party?
7. Who are your heroes?
8. What's the one thing about yourself you would most like to change?
9. What makes you proud about yourself?
10. What makes you different to everybody else?

Our values find expression in our accomplishments. Accomplishments are simple talking points, opening up new possibilities for conversation; they are evidence of experience and expertise that others might be looking for; they signal values to others without the need to spell them out.

It's not always easy to remember everything we've achieved, and it's not always obvious how our accomplishments might help others. If you make a list of your accomplishments, they will be ready in the background for you to use.

Expertise and accomplishments: a checklist

Make a note of what you are: *– and how these skills have helped you accomplish:*

good at   work projects

experienced with   sports activities

trained in   educational or training
                               courses

natural with   family or relationship
                               successes

successful in   volunteering or community
                               work.

It's up to you to acknowledge and celebrate your accomplishments. After all, only you know what they are! And when you start to talk about what you've achieved, you will begin to speak with passion about something you care about: always an infectious pleasure in conversation.

Create a self-introduction

We introduce ourselves to others so often that it's worth thinking about how to do it well. A self-introduction that develops rapport and generates interest can be one of our greatest networking assets.

Develop a self-introduction that you feel comfortable with. Practise different forms of words and see which ones trigger interest and intrigue. Which ones express your 'brand': your values and attitudes, as well as what you do?

Your self-introduction: a checklist

Keep it short
Your self-introduction should take no more than five seconds. Find the headline that summarises what you do in a single sentence.

Use a verb
State what you do – not what you are. Your introduction will be more dynamic and less ambiguous. 'I specialise in minor injuries at an A&E unit' is much more interesting than 'I'm a nurse'. 'I run training courses in communication skills' resolves the ambiguity of 'I'm a trainer'.

Be distinctive
What marks you out from others? What's different about what you do? What's unusual about the way you do business? What is the thing you really like doing?

Provide hooks
Use familiar language, not jargon or technical terms. Talk about what you do in terms of how other people experience it. Above all, keep using verbs: those 'doing' words will bring you alive in the other person's mind.

Engage
Beware the temptation to apologise for your existence! Smile; use clear and steady eye-contact; avoid words like 'just' and 'only' ('I'm just a secretary'; 'I'm only here because my manager asked me to come'). People will remember your warmth, your energy and your behaviour more than the words you use. Practise in front of a mirror, or with a friend. Do you *look* as if you mean what you are saying?

Many of us find it uncomfortable to 'blow our own trumpet'. But we don't need to play loudly or boisterously! People need to know what you have to offer, so that they can call on your talents. Quiet confidence and self-assurance are often more effective than blatant advertising.

Practice makes perfect. Practise being confident and professional; think about how to display your enthusiasm and energy. Try out your self-introduction at every opportunity. Ask trusted colleagues how you are doing. You are your own best public relations consultant. You know what you have to offer, and how good it is. You need to make it visible.

Marshal your resources

As with any other kind of communication, we have resources in three major areas that can help us. *Visual* resources include how we look and behave; our vocal resources are our voice and the parts of our body that support voice production; and verbal resources are the words we use.

If you marshal these resources *before* the event, you'll be better placed to use them during the event.

Visual resources

If you want to be perceived as professional, then you will need to look professional and behave professionally.

- *Think about your wardrobe.* **Build a clothes collection that represents your own values elegantly and simply. Buy a few, good-quality outfits that you can mix and match, rather than a lot of inferior-quality clothes. Darker colours generally work better than lighter shades: they hide stains and flatter the figure more effectively; and they tend to give an air of authority. If in doubt, dress *up* for the occasion; it's easy to adjust being** overdressed, but there's not much we can do on the spot to make up for being underdressed.

- *Use accessories wisely.* Learn how the extras can pull your image together. Jewellery, ties, scarves, bags, cases – they may project your brand more powerfully than your clothes. Coordination is key. A mix 'n' match approach may suggest the image of a scatterbrain.
- *Pay attention to grooming.* The state of your shoes, nails and hair matter. You're meeting people close up. It's worth thinking even about your breath.
- *Mind your manners.* How you stand, move and make eye contact, all say something about you. Pay attention to posture. The best thing you can wear is a smile.

Looks matter; and looking good is a mark of respect to the people you are meeting.

Vocal resources

The quality of your voice is also important. Volume, pace and pitch are the three core elements of our voice; we instinctively read a great deal about a person from our perceptions of these three vocal dimensions.

- *Make yourself heard.* You will probably be speaking against a babble of other voices. Direct your voice clearly at the other person; if they look as if they are straining to hear you, help by raising the volume a little.
- *Slow down.* Articulate clearly and don't gabble. Rushing your words will indicate nervousness or lack of interest. Use the breathing techniques mentioned in Chapter 7.
- *Lower your tone.* A thin, high-pitched voice will suggest a lack of authority or confidence. It's not easy to alter the tone of your voice convincingly; but if you breathe deeply and evenly, and feel your voice rising from the centre of your body rather than from a constricted throat, your tone will acquire strength and – well, body!

Beware also the irritating habit of 'uptalk': the creeping
tendency to end explanatory sentences on an upward
inflection, as if asking a question. (Its fancy name is the
'high-rising terminal'.)

- *Use your own accent.* Trying to fake a voice that is not
yours, or to alter your natural voice, is unnecessary. Be
proud of your voice: it is a vital component of your
identity. If your accent is distinct or strong, people may
have to work a little harder to adjust to your voice. So:
- *Speak clearly.* Make sure all the consonants are clear
when you are speaking (all the letters that are not A, E,
I, O or U). Use your lips and tongue well.

As with our other resources, we need to prepare our voice to
perform well. Practise in friendly situations; check how you are
doing with colleagues and friends whose opinion you trust.

Verbal resources

Among your verbal resources are your self-introduction and the
rapport-building remarks and questions. Listen, also, for the
words the other person is using and adjust your vocabulary to
theirs. Echoing the actual words a person uses can help to build
rapport very quickly, if done subtly.

Do you have a card?

Your business card is the trace you leave behind you. Its job is to
represent you in someone's memory after you have finished
talking. If they want to meet you again, your card is the means by
which they do it. Your card will – hopefully – be a permanent
reminder of you; it makes sense to get it right.

- *The card should reflect your 'brand'.* Does the design say
what you want it to say? Do the colours and typefaces

suggest your values and style? Are they compatible with your website or blog, if you have one?
- *Essential information should be easy to see.* Your name, your company, and the contact details should leap off the card.
- *Make use of space.* Don't clutter the card with unnecessary pictures or design features.
- *Quality pays.* Choose durable, good quality card. It's almost certainly worth having your card printed professionally, if you can afford it.

If you are new to the job market, or between jobs, take the trouble to create a new card containing your contact details. Handing out a card with outdated information is not a good idea – and makes an even worse impression if the information is hastily crossed out or overwritten. You may feel uncomfortable offering a stranger your address; a telephone number and e-mail address is quite sufficient.

Card games

Business cards can do more than represent you. They can themselves become sources of conversation.

What about the reverse of the card? It might be a useful place to put a slogan that develops your brand or style. You could leave it blank, or ruled with discreet lines, to encourage people to make notes about your conversation.

Have a supply of blank cards. They're useful for jotting down vital information (having a pen at the ready is a good idea, too!). You can use them yourself, and offer them to hapless contacts who find themselves without the necessary to make notes.

Decide how to store your cards. A cardholder looks more professional than a wad of cards in your breast pocket. A fancy cardholder can also be a talking point. Some people even carry two cardholders: one for their own cards, the other for cards they receive. People might be impressed to see their cards being stowed carefully in an elegant case.

How about a souvenir card? This is a card, exactly the same size as a business card, containing useful information relating to your business or work. An IT consultant might provide a card with little-known, instant computer fixes; a trainer might offer top tips for a key area they train. Souvenir cards make you more memorable; they build your brand; and they act as instant free gifts. They might even trigger a subliminal reciprocal response.

Look after your inner self

And it can still be hard work. Networking is exhausting and can be debilitating. After all, most of us meet a few new people every day; but few of us would find it entirely natural to meet dozens of new people in a couple of hours. Every new meeting is an opportunity, but it is also a challenge. We all need to look after ourselves before submitting to the next networking event.

Building up your confidence

However well we prepare, we may still lack the confidence to enter a room full of strangers. To counter the negativity, we often play little scenarios in our heads of all the things that could go wrong (or have gone wrong in the past), perhaps in the hope that this will prepare us better for the moments of danger. What we are actually doing is *rehearsing failure*.

Rehearsing failure is counterproductive. For a start, the more you rehearse failure, the better you will probably get at failing. Secondly, the more of these bad scenarios you run, the more stressed you will probably feel. When you are stressed, you can't learn, so you'll find it harder to change your behaviour.

If you *must* run mental movies of things going wrong, at least use a detached viewpoint. Imagine looking at a video of yourself behaving in this way, on a television screen. Imagine slowing the video down; carefully examine your behaviour and assess what you could do differently. 'Reframing' in this way tends to remove the emotional charge from your mental scenario.

Of course, a much better option than rehearsing failure is to rehearse success. This is not 'positive thinking'; it is running scenarios in our heads, in a carefully disciplined way, of ourselves behaving successfully.

Rehearsing success

1. Make yourself comfortable, in a quiet room, and close your eyes. Remove all distractions. (With a bit of practice, you'll find yourself being able to do this exercise just about anywhere. Be kind to yourself to start with.)

2. Imagine a television set. Set it down across the room and switch it on.

3. On the television screen, run a video of yourself performing well at a networking meeting. Watch the video carefully and notice what 'you' are doing. You can decide what you are watching; modify your imagined performance until you feel good (eager, excited or inspired).

4. Now adjust the video to make it really compelling. Bring up the sound; increase the screen size. Many people find that making it life-size, full colour, 3D, with surround-sound, works best.

5. Now, step into the movie so you are seeing the action through your own eyes, as if you were already there. Become aware of what you are *doing*, how you *look*, how you *sound* and how you *feel*.
6. Now step out again and shift your viewpoint a little way into the future beyond the event. Now you are looking back on it, taking notes and thinking about what you did well. Notice how you feel about it now.
7. Come back to now. Freeze-frame the video at a point where you can easily remember the image. That image will be your access point into the video, so that you can re-run it whenever you want.

Identifying goals

Now that you have prepared yourself, you need to set yourself clear goals for the networking event. Why are you attending, specifically? To make new friends? To look for new ideas? To create new relationships that might become new customers?

Working out your own goals

It's useful to think of your goals in terms of what you want, and what you want to give. Answer these questions carefully; write down your answers.

What do I want to gain? What do I want to give?

Make your answers positive. The answers should motivate you towards, not away from something.

How will I know when I have gained it? How will I know when I have given it?

Write down specifically the evidence telling you that you have achieved your goal. What information will you have? What promises will you have made, or secured?

Is my goal truly mine?

Have you chosen this goal? Is it something that you have

initiated? Sometimes we are set goals by our managers. If so, make sure you are happy with what you are being asked to achieve; negotiate if necessary, so that you feel in control of your goals. Be careful, also, to set only your own goals. We sometimes set goals for others: 'I want Peter to offer me a place in his team'; 'I want Marilyn to accept my offer of project support'. Concentrate on your own behaviour, not on others' actions.

What's the context?

Where will this goal take you? How does the goal for your networking event relate to your values, your strategy and your 'brand'? Are you willing to take on the responsibility that achieving the goal will give you? To give up what you might have to sacrifice to make the goal happen? Are you comfortable with this goal?

The skills of networking conversations

However much you prepare, the moment comes when you have to get going. You have to walk into the room and start talking to somebody.

There is no one way of doing this. Some people cannot resist starting with a humorous remark; others use well-established lines like: 'Have we met before?' or 'What brings you here?' The important thing is that you do it. Make contact.

Establishing rapport

Look back at the notes on building rapport in Chapter 1. Start positive or neutral. Complaining about the food is one way to make contact, but before long you may find yourselves agreeing that everything about the occasion is disastrous. Avoid emotive subjects such as religion and politics – at least to start with – and be very careful about assumptions linking one person with

another. 'Are you married?' can be an embarrassing opener – as I
found to my cost a few nights before writing this chapter.

Be appropriately vulnerable. The other person may well be
feeling as nervous as you are; acknowledging your own
apprehensions – especially if you go first – actually expresses
confidence and is an excellent free gift with which to start the
conversation.

It's more than likely that you won't remember the person's
name within the first few minutes of your conversation. Too
much else will be going on. A few simple tricks will help a name
to stick.

- *Use their name* on first introductions.

  Hi, I'm Megan.
  Megan, hi. Pleased to meet you. I'm Tony.

- *Ask for the name again if necessary.* **Taking the trouble to
  ask is another gift that will be appreciated.**
- *Use the other person's name once or twice during the
  conversation.* **Some people tend to be better at doing this
  than others; in my experience, Americans are more
  adept than Europeans at dropping your name into the
  conversation. It might feel a little awkward or false, but
  it will help you remember the name.**

Keeping the conversation going

In the early stages of a conversation, try to listen more than
speaking. Be the first to ask a question; then listen to the answer.
Make sure that it's an open question, beginning with one of the
six 'W's.

What do you do for a living?
Where do you meet most of your clients?
When did you start on this line of business?

Who is your link with the host organisation?
How did you start out?

Be careful with the question 'Why?' It's hard not to sound like an interrogator using that word, however hard you try.

Now listen for remarks that will generate another question. Have that question ready in the back of your mind as you listen on: you've solved the next move in the conversation and can relax a little!

Share something about yourself. (Remember the rule in Chapter 1: no more than three questions before you make a different kind of move.) Try to link your remark to what they have said. If you feel comfortable, shift the conversation to start discussing your aims for being there – and perhaps your aims for this conversation.

Summarise and paraphrase. Check your understanding of what the other person is saying; this keeps you focused, gives you time to think of something else to say and shows that you are listening.

Another way to keep the conversation going is to bring someone else in.

Chris, come and join us. We're just talking about...
I know who you should meet. Let me try to find Firoze...

'Passing the ball' in this way can relax or enhance a conversation. It can also be a good way to bring a conversation to a close politely: having introduced people to each other, you can excuse yourself and move on.

Joining groups

Approaching a group of people is slightly different from approaching an individual. People often worry about how to break into group conversations that are already in progress – and whether to do it. Being able to 'read' the group is helpful.

- *Arrive early.* One of the best ways to manage groups is to be in at the start of one.
- *Use previous contacts.* Everyone you speak to early in the event is a potential 'joiner' later: use one as a link person if you want to join a group.
- *Judge the tightness of the group.* How closely are people standing to each other? How is their eye contact? Can you see an opening, or is the group broadcasting its exclusivity by turning all backs on the rest of the room?
- *Exploit fractures.* Conversations rarely survive being extended beyond three people. Groups of four or more will either be audiences, listening to a single, dominant person, or mini-groups in the process of splintering from the main group. You could join the audience; or you could look for two people talking and gently insinuate yourself as a third.
- *Pick off stragglers.* Not everyone in the group will be entirely 'in the circle'. Find someone at the edge – perhaps they are looking as if they want an excuse to move on – and approach them.
- *Use listening time to establish your presence.* Make eye contact; respond to what someone is saying with smiles and nods. Ask a question as your first contribution: it's a good way to enter a conversation without being too rude.
- *Ask permission.* Find different ways of asking permission to enter new space.

Excuse me, I don't mean to interrupt, but I overheard you talking about...

Forgive me for interrupting, *but am I right in thinking that...*

Sorry to barge in, but can I just ask you about what you were saying?

'Playing host' is a brilliant way to break into groups. Pick up a bottle of wine or a plate of nibbles and circulate. Playing host is a great way to build rapport. You are putting people at their ease; you are offering gifts (always a great way to get people interested in you); you are able to introduce people to each other. Playing host also helps you: it gives you a certain authority (or at least something to do), and it gives you control. You can judge when to stay with someone and when to move on.

Pick someone who is alone!

One way to deal with the problem of breaking into groups is to start your own. Look out for someone who is on their own and looking uncomfortable. Approach them kindly and gently; share your own vulnerability. Use the occasion to exercise all your conversation skills. Draw in other people; introduce your new contact to someone you already know. Before you know it, you'll be the centre of a brilliant group conversation.

Closing the conversation

Whether the conversation has gone well, or not gone anywhere in particular, take care to close it well. The final impression we make is almost as important as the first one.

Never leave someone abruptly. A simple way to exit from a conversation is to connect the person to someone else in the room. Make the introduction; make sure that it has stuck (are they actually exchanging more than one remark with each other?); and walk away. Alternatively, use a plausible reason for leaving. Maybe you are expecting a colleague to arrive; maybe there is someone you need to speak to before they leave.

These are simple strategies for closing a conversation. But think a bit more deeply before you use them.

In Chapter 3, we looked at the WASP structure of conversation: **w**elcome, **a**cquire, **s**upply, **p**art. Make sure that the conversation covers every stage before moving on. What can you supply? Have you promoted yourself and your work clearly? What are the other person's needs? Ask: 'How can I help them?', 'Who do I know that might be of interest to them?'

Explore possibilities and opportunities. How could this person help you? Don't be afraid to share your needs and goals. Doors might open in the conversation that neither of you had previously noticed. The question 'Who do you know who ...?' can be a powerful networking question. Remember that you are networking to ask, not to demand. Even if they look like a good prospect, don't sell.

The parting stage of a conversation should always involve action of some sort. Lots of actions could end a conversation. You could:

- **invite the person to meet someone else;**
- **make a gift of information (or food, or drink...);**
- **agree to meet again; or**
- **exchange cards.**

Exchanging cards

The etiquette of exchanging business cards has become more sophisticated in recent years. Business cards are gifts; treat them as such and you won't go far wrong.

Keep your cards in good condition. This applies to cards you receive as well as your own. Business cardholders are a good idea; one for your own, one for cards offered. If someone gave you a gift, would you immediately stuff it away in your pocket?

Give your card respectfully. Choose who you offer your card to. Give your card when it's asked for; asking for a card is a compliment, so treat it as such. Ask permission to offer your card. If you give your card with respect, you will instil respect for yourself. Above all, don't leave a pile of cards on a table.

Receive cards with respect. The person offering is also paying a compliment, by trusting you with their contact details. Treat the card as a gift. Take it carefully; look at it; read it (aloud, perhaps); offer a compliment or a positive comment ('What an interesting design'; 'Ah, I see you're based in London'). Put the card away respectfully, perhaps only after you have parted.

It's a good idea to make notes on business cards: where you met, who introduced you, interesting information, agreed follow-up actions. However, you should never write on a business card in the other person's presence. (Unless they give you permission to do so, of course.)

The international etiquette of business cards

People are increasingly aware that business cards are handled differently in different cultures. One website offers the following advice.

Middle East

Always present your card with your right hand, never your left.

China

Have one side of your business card translated into Chinese and in gold-coloured lettering, as that is considered auspicious. If your company has been established for a very long time, it's useful to state the year it was formed on the card. When offering the card, you should do so with both hands.

Japan

To give and receive business cards in Japan is quite ceremonial. Status is important in Japan so make sure your title is prominent on the card. And, whilst it's perfectly acceptable to give your card with one hand, make sure you accept one with both hands. Keep it on the table in front of you. If you are meeting several people at once who have all given you their cards, keep all the cards on the table in front of you until the meeting has concluded. Place them in front of you in the order in which people are seated, to help you remember their names.

India

Business in India places a great emphasis on academic achievement. Your business cards should state any university qualifications you have, or any other kind of honour. As in the Middle East, always use your right hand when offering a business card.
(http://www.worketiquette.co.uk/business-card-etiquette-in-various-countries.html)

Following up and building your network

Don't waste the opportunities you have worked so hard for. Once you have made contact with people, think about how you can make use of that contact. Review your cards and notes at the end of the event. Record in your diary any obvious or immediate plans for follow-up. Don't let the cards gather dust in your case!

Recording contacts

Find a way of organising your network contacts that you find comfortable. Whether on card or electronic, your system must allow you to find contact details with a minimum of fuss. It should also be easy to review and adjust. If you can align your system to other systems you use for personal details – your personal organiser, your e-mail archives – so much the better.

Re-connecting with people

Having the contacts is of little use if you don't use them. There are lots of ways of re-connecting to people you have met.

Follow up fast. Send an e-mail within 24 hours. This is common courtesy and also establishes you on their e-mail system. Make the e-mail personal; no round robins and no copying in.

Include a gift. Pick up on the conversation you were holding and offer anything that you think might be of interest. Typically, this will be more information: documents (brochures, e-newsletters), links, or contact details for other people.

Invite them to make contact. It might be lunch; or a phone call; or another event where you could meet on neutral ground.

Avoid fatigue and annoyance. If someone doesn't reply, manage future contacts with care. Plan further 'nudges' over a period of weeks or months.

Asking for help

A very good way to re-connect is to ask for help. If there is something that the contact can do to assist you, invite them to offer it. It's flattering to be asked to give something. Make sure that you balance your requests with regular offers. (See the notes on the 'Netbank', below.)

'Joining the dots'

One of the most valuable gifts we can offer in business is contacts with other people. Generosity tends to beget generosity.

The general rule is to be carefully generous. Offer safe contact details: an e-mail address should be sufficient. If you're uncertain, check with the third person that they are happy to have their details passed on.

Constructing a network map

You could go further. Constructing a map of your network (or networks!) might help you get more value from them. In particular, they can help you find cross-connections between people in different parts of your life.

You could create network maps on paper, or using software such as MindManager or The Brain. With yourself at the hub of the map, draw links to various categories: 'Family', 'Community', 'Education', 'Work', 'Music', 'Clubs', 'Friends', and so on. Now add individuals to those categories that you know personally: people you would feel happy cold-calling on the phone. Add links to people that you know that *they* know, or people that you are weakly tied to in some way. You could begin to add notes, colour coding and other visual effects to develop patterns or clusters of contacts (MindManager has plenty of functions to help you).

The trick in creating this network map is to concentrate on the *weak* ties. People with strong ties to you will tend to share your interests, expertise and contacts. People with weak ties have access to new information, resources and people; they are the ones who will help you most to grow and enrich your network. (The sociologist Mark Granovetter coined the phrase 'the strength of weak ties' to capture this idea.)

Keeping the connections alive

Think of your network as an organism. It is alive, continually shape-shifting and adapting itself to your environment: your personal circumstances, your work patterns, your ambitions and desires. Like any organism, it needs to be healthy to survive and grow: it needs feeding, nurturing, exercise – and occasional pruning. Review your network regularly: perhaps once a year. Check contact details and clean out the system; move people around; make new connections. Ask how you can enliven contacts that have 'gone to sleep' for a while; think about how new relationships can help you in new ways.

In particular, look for the 'connectors'. Connectors have what Prince Charles calls 'convening power'. These are people who can act as mediators or 'honest brokers', putting people in contact with each other for mutual benefit. Ask how a connector could help you fulfil a need, and what would be in it for them.

The Netbank

We have a 'net account' with everyone in our network. Just like a real bank account, our net accounts with people can be in credit or overdrawn. (Whenever we say 'I'm in your debt', or 'I'm obliged', we are signalling the need to balance our net account with someone.)

Diane Darling suggests that the best way to check our net balance with someone is to try to make a withdrawal.

- When you need to call them, will you feel comfortable doing so?
- How long has it been since you put something into the account?
- The last time they asked you to help, did you do so?

If you think your net account with someone is dangerously low, make a deposit.

- Find something you can do for the person.
- Don't ask them for anything.

- Identify people with whom you are in 'net credit'. Could they help you with a 'net loan'?

  Remember that deposits gather 'net interest'. A small deposit can quickly garner bigger returns.

Volunteering

Networking is a proactive business. Waiting for the phone to ring is not the way to do it. Get out there and exercise your communication skills; put yourself about; make yourself known.

Use your organisation's facilities. Most organisations have employee networks, and social or activity-based groups that you can use to make new friends and useful contacts. Be guided by your interests, and network from your centre. Avoid whatever seems superficial or uncomfortable.

Start your own network. If an area of interest or a constituency seems under-represented in your organisation, start a new network. Think about who might help you run it; look for sponsorship at senior levels; promote the network boldly. It's important that networks should not be seen as divisive or exclusive. The whole point is to bring people together, not drive them apart.

Organise a networking event. If you are responsible for setting up an event where people will be networking, you can do a great deal to make it easier for people to meet.

Volunteer. Put yourself forward to speak at meetings or conferences. Offer to chair meetings and to join committees. Become an author: editors of newsletters and magazines are often desperate for new providers of copy.

Cross boundaries. Look beyond your organisation, to cross-industry organisations, and groups with shared intellectual or professional interests. Look at your network map and think about organisations linked to people you know – and to your weak ties, in particular.

Speed-networking: a proposal

Erica Munro is a writer who understands the necessity of networking while hating the word. In an amusing article on her website, she suggests a simple way to make networking palatable. It's designed along the speed-dating principle and it would go like this:

1. The word 'networking' would be banned.
2. So would warm white wine.
3. Also out – any suggestion that it's a social event. This is business. It would take place during the day, for a start, so as not to cut into precious evening time with family and friends.
4. The event would be split in two. First, everyone takes a number, a notebook, and a pen.
5. Then everyone takes their turn to stand up and say who they are, what they do and what information they're looking to get out of the event. About 40 seconds each should do it.
6. The others all make notes.
7. When everyone is finished, participants head for the person or people who may be of use to them.

At last, it's speed-networking time. Name, rank, serial number, business card – all exchanged within a five-minute slot, with a little bell denoting when it's time to shake hands and move on.

Exploring

Effective networkers go sideways. They use every opportunity to practise their networking skills and seek new relationships.

Don't have a goal. Displaying a sense of purpose when networking usually kills it stone dead. Effective networking is about giving with no thought of any return. If you get nothing out of it, move on. But on most occasions, giving *does* give you a return.

Use the 'three-foot rule'. Everyone within a metre of you is potentially a conversation partner. This is because they are entering what Edward T Hall calls our 'personal space': the space we usually reserve for our friends. Go through a day noticing who comes into your personal space. Be ready to make eye contact and to say 'hello'. Find the friendly remark that might trigger conversation. Don't force people to talk to you, or put them under any obligation to you. Give, and see what happens. Notice what works and move on.

Trains and planes

Some of our most memorable conversations can be with strangers when travelling. Something about the neutral space of an airport or railway station makes it easier for us to reach out to people. Here are some tips on making the most of travelling time.

Carry a book or a music player. This shows that you are not desperate to talk – and offers an escape route if the person turns out to be difficult or boring. A book can also be a conversation starter.

When you sit down near another person, smile and greet them. Notice their response.

Respect the other person's personal space – especially when it is constricted (particularly important on aircraft!).

Offer help – luggage, directions, useful information. This is a great way to break the ice. But don't expect anything in return!

> **Observe body language.** If the person isn't interested in talking, their body will tell you so.
> **Show interest.** Ask a question and show appreciation of the answer. We all love to feel that we have taught someone something!

Find new ways of making your voice heard. People now keep in touch in a host of ways: social networking sites, e-mail, instant messaging, blogging... Think about how you can use electronic media to promote your messages and offer useful gifts to people in your network.

Regularly look at things differently. This is not a matter of simply 'thinking outside the box'. Use some simple disciplines to nudge your thinking into new areas. Deliberately ask key questions, such as:

- **How else could I view this relationship?**
- **How do they see me?**
- **What don't they know about me?**
- **Who else would be interested in this?**
- **How else could I present this idea?**
- **Where else would this work?**
- **What would this look like in a completely different business sector?**

We often need help simply seeing our situation in fresh ways. Who are the trusted friends in your network who could help you get a fresh perspective?

Follow your bliss. What really interests you? What is your intuition telling you? If you don't act on your hunches, you'll never know whether there was something there.

The ten commandments of effective networking

1. You get what you give.
2. Be yourself.
3. Honour your relationships.
4. Share; don't hoard.
5. Ask for what you want.
6. Promote yourself professionally.
7. Move on when necessary.
8. Record all your contacts.
9. Follow up.
10. Expand your horizons.

Appendix: where to go from here

Communication is continuous, and we never finish learning how to improve. My blog explores issues and events relating to the material in this book. You can find it at: http://justwriteonline. typepad.com/distributed_intelligence/. Here are some thoughts about books and other resources that will take further the ideas we have explored in this book.

Chapter 1: What is communication?

The fullest explanation I have found of the Shannon–Weaver model of communication is on Mick Underwood's magnificent (and award-winning) website: http://www.cultsock.ndirect.co.uk/index2.html.

I also found David Chandler's page useful: http://www.aber. ac.uk/media/Documents/short/trans.html#N.

The four principles of communication are based on ideas by Donnell King. Find them at: http://www.pstcc.edu/facstaff/dking/interpr.htm.

Steven Mithen's book *The Prehistory of the Mind* (Phoenix, London, 1998) discusses the origins of communication in primate activity. Margaret Wheatley's *Leadership and the New Science* (Berret-Koehler, San Francisco, 1992) brings insights from quantum theory and complexity to bear on ideas of information.

Chapter 2: How conversations work

Peter Senge's book *The Fifth Discipline* (Random House, London, 2nd edn, 2006) relates conversation to systems theory. William Isaac's *Dialogue and the Art of Thinking Together* (Currency Books, New York, 1999) is at the leading edge of studies into conversation.

Chapter 3: Seven ways to improve your conversations

First- and second-stage thinking are notions that inform Edward de Bono's work. Look at *Lateral Thinking in Management* (Penguin, London, 1982). The four types of conversation derive from the work of Michael Wallacek, who may have been influenced by Werner Erhard.

Chris Argyris' Ladder of Inference is best found in *The Fifth Discipline Fieldbook*, edited by Peter Senge and others (Nicholas Brealey, London, 1994).

For more on mindmaps, see Tony Buzan's *Use your Head* (BBC, London, 1974).

Chapter 4: The skills of enquiry

Nancy Kline's *Time to Think* (Ward Lock, London, 1999) is a fascinating study of deep listening.

Chapter 5: The skills of persuasion

Peter Thompson's *Persuading Aristotle* (Kogan Page, London, 1999) relates classical rhetoric to modern business techniques entertainingly. For more on pyramids, look at Barbara Minto's *The Pyramid Principle* (Pitman, London, 1987).

Chapter 6: Interviews: holding a formal conversation

Alan Barker's *How to be Better at Managing People* (Kogan Page, London, 2000) discusses all of these types of interview, and other kinds of managerial conversation, in more depth.

For more on coaching, John Whitmore's *Coaching for Performance* (Nicholas Brealey, London, 1992) is a central text. Reg Hamilton's *Mentoring* (Industrial Society, London, 1993) contains some useful material on counselling.

Chapter 7: Making a presentation

Max Atkinson's book *Lend Me Your Ears* (Vermilion, London, 2004) takes a strikingly new approach to the subject of presenting and speech-writing.

Chapter 8: Putting it in writing

Alan Barker's *Writing at Work* (Industrial Society, London, 1999) is a comprehensive guide to writing business documents.

Chapter 9: Networking: the new conversation

Two books taking usefully complementary approaches to networking are Steven D'Souza's *Brilliant Networking* (Pearson Education, Harlow, 2008), and *Power Networking* by Donna Fisher and Sandy Vilas (Bard Press, Atlanta, USA, 2000).